Mastering Co-Regulation Parenting:

Enhance Emotional Intelligence, Achieve Peaceful, Harmonious Family Relationships and Build Effective Stress Management Skills

Written By
Sarah Libby

Dedication

To Dana—

Your unwavering love, patience, and partnership are the steady
ground beneath my feet. Thank you for always believing in me.

To Nathan and Joshua—

You are my greatest teachers and my deepest inspiration. This book
is for you and because of you.

With all my heart, I love you.

About The Author

Sarah Libby is a compassionate 45-year-old mother of two who is deeply passionate about her work, specializing in co-regulation and emotional connection.

With over two decades of experience as a special education teacher, Sarah brings a wealth of insight into child development, emotional regulation, and the unique needs of neurodiverse learners. Her deep understanding of how children learn, communicate, and connect fuels her commitment to helping families build stronger, more empathetic relationships.

Sarah offers practical, heart-centered strategies that guide parents through everyday challenges with calm, clarity, and compassion. Drawing on her professional expertise and personal journey as a mother, she shares tools and perspectives that support caregivers in building emotionally secure, connected relationships with their children.

She aims to help families create nurturing environments where children feel seen, heard, and understood. Sarah's approachable, empowering style has made her a trusted resource for those seeking to raise emotionally resilient and confident kids.

Introduction

Every day, countless parents find themselves in a familiar scenario: the morning rush, where emotions run high, patience wears thin, and both parent and child feel frazzled and disconnected. The seemingly endless battle against stress and miscommunication is a common challenge. But what if there were practical, research-backed methods to manage and transform these moments into opportunities for emotional growth and more profound connection? This is where the journey of co-regulating parenting begins.

My name is Sarah Libby, and I have devoted my career to exploring the dynamics of parent-child relationships, focusing on emotional intelligence and stress management. Every parent and child can form a loving and emotionally intelligent bond. With my background in education and psychology, I blend the latest research with practical, accessible strategies designed to shift the parenting paradigm from reactive to proactive, from isolated to interconnected. Emotional co-regulation is not just a professional pursuit for me; it's personal. I've experienced the transformative power of co-regulation parenting in my relationship with my son, Joshua, and I'm excited to share these insights with you.

Co-regulation refers to how a parent and child manage their emotional states together, not just side by side but integrated. This approach is not just about calming down; it's about building a foundation of mutual understanding and respect that enhances emotional intelligence across the family unit. The significance of co-regulation lies in its power to foster an environment where peace and harmony are the norms, not the exceptions. By practicing co-regulation parenting, you can expect a significant reduction in stress and conflict within your family and a noticeable increase in emotional intelligence and understanding.

In "Mastering Co-Regulation Parenting," you will embark on a journey to enhance your emotional intelligence and that of your children. This book's transformative goals are within your reach—to create more peaceful, harmonious family relationships and to equip you with effective stress management skills. Through practical, easy-to-implement strategies, you will learn how to apply co-regulation principles in everyday life, turning challenging interactions into powerful opportunities for growth and connection.

The structure of this book is not just about theory; it's about practical application. It will guide you from foundational concepts to advanced strategies and real-world applications. Each chapter builds on the previous one, ensuring a smooth progression that enriches your understanding and skills as you progress. The book remains grounded in practicality by addressing real-life scenarios you face daily, making each lesson relevant and immediately applicable.

I understand your struggles and aspirations as a parent. We all yearn for a deep, meaningful connection with our children; sometimes, despite our best intentions, we feel stuck. I've been there in both my professional practice and personal experiences. I vividly remember when my son, Joshua, was around three years old, and he had a massive meltdown over his father leaving the house and not taking him with him. At that point, I was knee-deep in parenting books, trying to figure out the best strategies for handling tantrums. But none of the advice seemed to work in the heat of the moment. In this moment of desperation, I discovered the power of co-regulation parenting. Instead of trying to reason with him or enforce consequences, I decided to try something different. I sat beside him, wrapped my arms around him, and took deep breaths. I gently whispered, "It's okay, baby. I'm here with you." Initially, he resisted, still caught up in his frustration. But gradually, as I breathed calmly and held him close, he relaxed. His cries softened, and he leaned into me, seeking comfort. In that moment, I realized the power of co-regulation. By staying calm and providing a safe space for his emotions, I was able to help him regulate his feelings. It wasn't about fixing the problem immediately or dismissing his emotions; it was about being present and showing him that he wasn't alone in his struggles. From then on, whenever tantrums arose, I consciously prioritized connection and empathy over discipline. And each time, I saw how our bond grew more substantial, and Joshua became more adept at managing his emotions with my support. It was a pivotal moment in my parenting journey, teaching me the invaluable lesson that sometimes the best way to help our children is to be there for them, offering love and understanding.

This book invites you to embrace a transformative approach to parenting that values emotional connection and intelligent interaction. It's written for you, with straightforward strategies grounded in current research yet easy to integrate into your daily life. You don't need a degree in psychology to apply these principles; you need an open heart and a willingness to grow.

As you turn these pages, remember that mastering co-regulation parenting is a journey that evolves with you and your family. I encourage you to revisit concepts and strategies as you encounter new parenting stages and challenges. Let's embrace the potential for change, peace, and a deeper, more harmonious connection with our children. Let's start this transformative journey today.

Table of Contents

Chapter 1:
Understanding Co-Regulation

Have you ever noticed how a baby's heartbeat calms when cradled close to their parent? Or how a toddler's tantrum subsides with a soothing tone of voice? These moments, rooted in the science of emotional co-regulation, are not just advantageous; they are transformative. As a parent, understanding the underpinnings of this process is not just a step but a leap toward transforming your relationship with your child into a harmonious bond. This chapter will delve into the profound connection between neuroscience and everyday parenting interactions. Here, you will discover how your emotional state directly influences your child's and how, through science-backed strategies, you can foster an environment of mutual understanding and emotional growth.

1.1 The Science Behind Emotional Co-Regulation: Unveiling the Brain's Role

Understanding the Neuroscience

The brain, our intricate organ, plays a central role in regulating emotions. The limbic system, often called the 'emotional brain,' is crucial in emotional processing. It includes structures such as the amygdala, hippocampus, and hypothalamus, which process and interpret emotional responses together. A key aspect of its function is how it interacts with mirror neurons, cells that react when we observe the same action performed by someone else. These neurons are foundational in developing empathy and understanding within social interactions. As a parent, your emotional state directly influences your child's. When you express calmness during a stressful situation, your child's mirror neurons activate, mimicking this emotional state, thereby promoting a calm response in your child. This mirroring effect is a cornerstone of effective co-regulation, illustrating how closely tied our emotional states are to those we are in close contact with, especially between parent and child.

Biological Sync between Parent and Child

The physical closeness between you and your child can do more than provide comfort; it can synchronize your physiological states, including heart rates and emotional responses. This biological synchronization helps in forming a secure attachment and enhances emotional bonding. Research in developmental psychology suggests that such synchrony can lead to better emotional regulation in children as they grow. When a parent consistently responds to a child's needs in a sensitive and nurturing manner, it not only soothes the child in that moment but also teaches them how to regulate their emotions over time.

Impact of Secure Attachment

When caregivers provide reliable comfort and security, children form a secure attachment. This form of attachment is not just a momentary comfort but a crucial foundation for effective co-regulation. It establishes a 'safe base' from which children explore their environment and learn new skills. The security that comes from this attachment enables children to handle stress better because they know they have a safe emotional refuge in their parents. Studies have shown that securely attached children are likelier to have improved problem-solving skills, better emotional health, and stronger peer relationships than those with insecure attachments. This underscores the importance of nurturing a responsive and empathetic parenting style, as it can have long-lasting positive effects on your child's emotional development.

Stress Response Systems

The way you handle stress has a profound impact on how your child manages stress as well. When faced with stress, every individual, adult or child, experiences activation of their body's stress response systems, notably the hypothalamic-pituitary-adrenal (HPA) axis, which regulates cortisol, the stress hormone. Your calm demeanor is not just a regulatory mechanism; it's a powerful tool that helps modulate the child's stress responses. For example, when children see their parents handling a stressful situation calmly, their physiological stress response is attenuated, promoting a sense of security and teaching them to respond similarly in stressful situations. This form of modeling is not just crucial; it's effective in helping your child develop resilience to stress.

Understanding these aspects of emotional co-regulation provides insight into the physiological and emotional dynamics between you and your child and equips you with knowledge to enhance these interactions. By applying these principles, you can nurture emotional health and manage stressful situations confidently and calmly.

1.2 The Art of Synchronizing Emotions: Parent and Child as Partners

Emotional Attunement

At the heart of a synchronized relationship between you and your child lies the art of emotional attunement. That art involves tuning into each other's emotional frequencies without words through facial expressions, body posture, and even the tone of voice. Think of it like a silent conversation where much is said without speaking. For parents, this means observing and interpreting their child's nonverbal signals and responding in a way that conveys understanding and empathy. This two-way emotional exchange is pivotal. When children feel understood, they are more likely to open up and share their deeper feelings and thoughts, fostering a trust-based relationship. If your child hunches their shoulders and casts down their gaze, it may indicate that they feel sad or discouraged. Sit beside them, match their quiet tone, and gently encourage them to share their thoughts, showing you are present and attentive. Over time, this practice helps your child develop the trust necessary to express their emotions more freely and teaches them that their feelings are valid and essential. This emotional exchange is about problem-solving and nurturing an environment where emotions are respected and valued, setting the stage for deeper emotional connections.

The Dance of Co-Regulation

Describing co-regulation as a dance is a fitting metaphor, encapsulating this dynamic and interactive process. In this dance, you and your child take turns leading and following, continuously adjusting to each other's emotional cues. Just as in dance, where partners respond to subtle signals, weight shifts, and changes in rhythm, co-regulation involves responding to shifts in emotional states and needs. This reciprocal adjustment is what makes co-regulation a fluid and evolving process. One day, you might find that maintaining calm helps soothe your child's anxieties, while another, you might follow your child's lead, embracing their joy in a moment of spontaneous play. Each step in this dance builds on mutual respect and understanding, reinforcing a resilient and adaptive bond. This dynamic process teaches children that relationships involve give and take, that their emotions impact others, and that they also have a role in maintaining the emotional balance in the family.

Modeling Emotional Regulation

As a parent, you are your child's first and most influential teacher, and one of the most crucial lessons you impart is how to manage emotions. Modeling emotional regulation is not about suppressing feelings but expressing them in healthy and constructive ways. Children learn to emulate these behaviors When they observe their parents handling disappointment with grace or managing anger with techniques like deep breathing or taking a timeout. It's crucial to narrate your process of emotional regulation as it happens. For instance, if you're feeling overwhelmed by a situation, you might say, "I'm feeling frustrated right now, so I'm going to take a few deep breaths to calm down." Modeling this not only shows your child a practical method of managing heavy emotions but also normalizes the experience of feeling overwhelmed, teaching them that seeking calm is a natural and positive step. This ongoing demonstration of emotional regulation provides children with a real-time playbook on how to handle their emotions, significantly impacting their ability to manage their feelings in immediate and future contexts.

Shared Joy and Sorrow

Sharing emotions, be they joyous or sorrowful, creates a fabric of shared experiences that strengthens the emotional bonds within a family. Celebrating achievements and joys together, like a job well done on a school project or excitement over a family holiday, reinforces a sense of unity and belonging. Similarly, sharing in the sorrows, such as consoling each other during times of loss or disappointment, solidifies a support system within the family. Creating spaces where these emotions can be expressed openly and without judgment is crucial. For example, encourage sharing the highs and lows of the week during family gatherings, allowing each family member, regardless of age, to articulate their triumphs and struggles. This practice normalizes the expression of a wide range of emotions and teaches empathy as family members resonate with and support each other's emotional expressions. Ensuring such practices multiply joy and divide sorrow reinforces the co-regulatory framework where we manage emotions collectively and compassionately.

1.3 Decoding Emotional Signals: A Guide to Understanding Your Child's Emotional Language

Recognizing Nonverbal Cues

Children, especially in their early years, rely heavily on nonverbal cues to express their emotions and needs. As a parent, developing the ability to interpret these cues, be it a furrowed brow, averted gaze, or the clenching of fists, can significantly enhance your understanding of your child's emotional state. For instance, consider a scenario where a young child returns from school appearing sullen with shoulders slumped and eyes downcast. Such body language might indicate sadness or disappointment, perhaps due to a troubling interaction with peers or a difficult day at school. By recognizing these subtle nonverbal expressions, you can proactively address the underlying emotions, open a dialogue to discuss their feelings or offer a comforting hug. Observing these cues in context is essential, as the same signs could mean different things depending on the situation. A child's clenched fists during play might express excitement, whereas the same gesture at the dinner table might signal frustration or resistance to the meal. Enhancing your observational skills can help you respond more effectively to your child's emotional needs, making them feel seen and understood even before exchanging a word.

The Importance of Active Listening

This skill is crucial in validating your child's feelings and encouraging open communication. It requires you to be fully present, putting aside your thoughts and judgments, to hear your child and understand what they are trying to convey. This form of listening might mean getting down to your child's eye level and maintaining gentle eye contact, which conveys that you are engaged and attentive. For example, when your child talks about their day, instead of offering immediate advice or solutions, you might reflect on what you've heard, saying, "It sounds like you had a tough time when your friend wouldn't share the toy with you." Such reflections show that you are listening and help clarify and deepen your understanding of your child's feelings. Active listening fosters a trusting environment where children feel safe to express their thoughts and emotions, knowing they will be received with empathy and without immediate judgment or rectification.

Emotional Vocabulary Development

Developing a rich emotional vocabulary is a fundamental aspect of emotional intelligence. It allows children to articulate their feelings clearly, which is essential for practical, emotional expression and regulation. Children benefit from being taught specific words to describe a wide range of emotions from a young age. This education can begin with more simplistic labels like "happy," "sad," "angry," and "scared" and expand to more nuanced terms like "frustrated," "lonely," "excited," and "nervous" as they grow. Engaging in daily conversations that involve expressing your own emotions using specific vocabulary can model this behavior. For instance, instead of saying you had a bad day, you might express, "I felt frustrated today because my meeting didn't go as planned," or "I'm proud of you for helping your friend; it shows kindness." Books are also a fantastic resource for building emotional vocabulary; stories are full of characters experiencing different emotions, providing natural opportunities for discussion. Asking open-ended questions like, "How do you think this character felt when that happened?" helps children connect words to emotions, reinforcing their understanding and ability to express them accurately.

Responding to Emotions Appropriately

Understanding your child's emotions is one thing; responding to them in a way that fosters emotional growth and connection is another. Each emotion your child experiences and expresses offers an opportunity for teaching and connection. The key is to respond in ways that validate their feelings while guiding them toward managing those emotions constructively. For example, if your child is angry because they have to stop playing to do homework, dismissing their anger with "Don't be silly, just do your homework" might make them feel misunderstood and less likely to share their feelings in the future. Instead, acknowledging their emotion with a response like, "I see you're upset about having to stop playing. It's okay to feel angry, but let's figure out how we can finish the homework and get back to playing," helps them understand that their emotions are acceptable. It also teaches them how to transition from feeling to action positively. This approach respects their feelings and helps them learn to deal with disappointments and disruptions, which are inevitable parts of life. By consistently responding to your child's emotions with empathy and support, you reinforce their ability to manage emotions independently and build a strong foundation for emotional intelligence.

1.4 The Impact of Stress on Parent-Child Dynamics: Navigating Emotional Storms Together

Understanding how stress manifests in children is pivotal to fostering a supportive, nurturing environment that encourages healthy emotional development. Stress in children can often appear as changes in behavior, such as increased irritability, withdrawal from social interactions, or changes in eating and sleeping patterns, which might initially be difficult to link directly to stress. Younger children, lacking the verbal skills to express their feelings, might revert to thumb-sucking or clinging to a comfort object. Older children might display stress through anger, defiance, or declining school performance. These behaviors are symptomatic of the underlying stress and are often a child's way of signaling discomfort or anxiety about situations they find overwhelming or confusing.

The sources of stress in children are as varied as the children themselves. They range from changes in routine, conflicts with peers, and academic pressures to family issues such as parental discord or financial troubles. Each stressor impacts children differently, and understanding these sources is the first step in mitigating their effects. The impact of stress on a child's ability to regulate their emotions is significant. Stress triggers the body's flight-or-fight response, flooding the system with hormones such as adrenaline and cortisol. This biological response can make calm, measured responses to everyday challenges more complex, leading to behaviors that can strain the parent-child dynamic.

To effectively support their children, parents must first manage their stress. Managing stress is beneficial for the parent and crucial for the child. Children are highly perceptive and often pick up on the emotional states of their parents, and a stressed parent can inadvertently amplify a child's anxiety. Techniques for managing parental stress are numerous, but they all start with self-awareness. Recognizing your signs of stress is vital to handling it effectively. Techniques such as deep breathing exercises, mindfulness meditation, or simply engaging in a hobby can significantly reduce stress levels. For instance, setting aside time each day for a quiet activity you enjoy, reading, gardening, or yoga, can provide a valuable break and reduce overall stress levels. This practice not only aids your emotional regulation but also models healthy stress management for your children.

Creating a calming environment at home plays a crucial role in reducing stress triggers for you and your child. This environment involves both physical and emotional aspects. Physically, a cluttered, chaotic home environment can mirror and even enhance feelings of stress. Simple routines that keep living spaces orderly and predictable can alleviate this stress. Emotionally, a home where feelings are respected and open communication is encouraged is inherently calming. Establish routines that foster calm, especially during transitions, which are often stress points in a child's day. For example, a bedtime routine that includes winding down activities like reading a story or listening to soft music can help ease the transition to sleep, a time often fraught with resistance from children.

Joint stress-reduction techniques can further enhance the parent-child bond while managing stress. Engaging in activities that both parent and child find relaxing can be a fun and effective way to reduce stress. Mindfulness practices, such as guided imagery or joint breathing exercises, offer simple, effective methods to calm the nervous system and foster a sense of safety and connection. For instance, spending a few minutes each evening doing a breathing exercise together helps calm the physiological stress response and strengthens the emotional connection. Shared hobbies, such as painting, hiking, or cooking, can also be excellent stress relievers that build lasting bonds. These activities provide opportunities for conversations that might not happen in the busier moments of the day and allow both parent and child to explore new facets of their relationship in a relaxed setting.

Navigating the complexities of stress in the parent-child dynamic requires understanding, patience, and proactive strategies. By recognizing the signs of stress, managing personal stress effectively, creating a calming environment, and engaging in joint stress-reduction activities, you can help ensure that stress does not overwhelm your family's dynamic but becomes a catalyst for strengthening your bonds and enhancing emotional resilience.

1.5 Building the Emotional Intelligence Bridge: Strategies for Enhancing EQ in the Family

Emotional intelligence (EQ) is the cornerstone of personal success and healthy, resilient relationships. EQ can transform interactions within the family and foster an environment where every member thrives emotionally and socially. Emotional intelligence involves understanding one's emotions, empathizing with others, and effectively managing emotional responses to life's challenges. Developing this in a family setting means creating daily practices that cultivate awareness, empathy, and resilience.

One effective way to enhance EQ in the family is through shared activities focusing on developing emotional awareness and expression. Emotion-focused storytelling, for example, can be a powerful tool. This involves telling stories where characters navigate various emotions and face scenarios requiring emotional resilience. After reading a book, discuss with your children what the characters might have felt during significant events. Please encourage them to think about how they would feel in similar situations and explore different ways the characters could manage their emotions. Perspective-taking helps children understand and label emotions accurately and enhances their empathy by putting themselves in someone else's shoes.

Incorporating games that require emotional intelligence can also be beneficial. Games like 'emotion charades,' where family members act out different emotions for others to guess, can make learning about emotions fun and engaging. This helps younger children recognize and name emotions and enhances their ability to read emotional cues, a critical aspect of developing EQ. For older children and adults, games that involve moral dilemmas or decision-making can stimulate discussions about emotional responses and the consequences of various actions, providing deeper insights into managing emotions in complex situations.

Empathy training within the family is another crucial element in building emotional intelligence. Exercises that focus on understanding and sharing the feelings of others can be very beneficial. One such exercise is the 'emotion day' where each family member picks an emotion and acts it out during the day, and others must respond appropriately. For instance, if someone chooses 'frustration,' they might exhibit signs of frustration, and family members would use this as a cue to offer support or help. This exercise helps recognize and respond to emotional cues and understand what behaviors might help alleviate or enhance negative emotions.

One cannot overstate the importance of feedback in emotional growth. Constructive feedback helps individuals understand how their behavior affects others, fostering greater self-awareness and empathy. In a family setting, it is vital to establish a culture where feedback is given and received in a supportive manner. For instance, after a conflict, discuss the feelings experienced during the disagreement and provide input on how to handle similar situations differently in the future. Focus on using 'I' statements, such as "I felt ignored when you walked away while I was talking," rather than accusatory 'you' statements, which can lead to defensiveness. Open and honest communication helps family members understand each other's emotional responses and learn from interactions.

Emotional intelligence is more than just handling emotions effectively; it's about building a foundation for more robust and empathetic relationships. Families can cultivate an environment where emotional intelligence is valued and continuously enhanced through daily practices and dedicated activities. Focusing on these areas ensures that your family understands emotions and grows together in emotional wisdom. This growth is essential, not just for personal success but for nurturing a family dynamic that is supportive, resilient, and deeply connected.

Chapter 2:
Implementing Co-Regulation Strategies

Imagine you are crafting a sanctuary, a space where every corner, every moment spent, is a reassurance of safety and understanding. This place isn't just any place; it's your home, the heart where family emotions ebb and flow. Creating a safe emotional space is essential in nurturing co-regulation. It forms the very foundation of trust and openness in the parent-child relationship. As you delve into this chapter, picture yourself weaving a tapestry of security and warmth, where each thread represents an action or a word dedicated to enhancing emotional safety.

2.1 Creating a Safe Emotional Space: The Heart of Co-Regulation

The Importance of Safety

The towering structure of your child's emotional and psychological well-being is built upon the cornerstone of safety, particularly emotional safety. The fertile soil nurtures the roots of trust and openness, allowing the delicate buds of vulnerability to bloom without fear. When children feel safe, they are more likely to share their innermost feelings, seek comfort, and express themselves without fearing judgment or reprisal. This safety is crucial in co-regulation, where the shared management of emotions can only thrive in an environment where both parent and child feel secure enough to be their true selves. Emotional safety fosters a deep-seated bond, a secure attachment from which children derive the confidence to explore the world and the sanctuary to which they return.

Techniques for Creating Safety

Creating an emotionally safe environment involves more than love and good intentions; it requires conscious, consistent actions and decisions. Start by cultivating a non-judgmental, accepting atmosphere where all emotions are allowed and respected. This means listening to your child's frustrations with school just as attentively as you celebrate their successes. It involves acknowledging their fears about the dark and their excitement for a family outing. Another powerful technique is the use of affirming language and supportive body language. Phrases like "I'm here for you" or "It's okay to feel scared," paired with a comforting hug or a reassuring smile, can significantly enhance feelings of safety and acceptance. Additionally, consider the power of presence by simply being fully engaged and attentive with your child can communicate safety more profoundly than words.

Physical Environment Matters

The physical environment is pivotal in creating a sense of security and belonging. This environment can be simple: a cozy corner with cushions and blankets for quiet time or a special nook with their favorite books and toys. Such spaces provide a physical sanctuary where children can retreat and regroup, offering a sensory experience of safety. Lighting, colors, and decor should evoke calmness and warmth. Soft lighting, soothing colors like blues and greens, and personal touches like family photos or artwork can transform a space into a comforting haven. This physical environment acts as a safe base, a tangible representation of the emotional safety you cultivate through interactions.

Consistency and Predictability

Children thrive on consistency and predictability; these elements breed security and trust. When children know what to expect, they feel in control and safe. This can be as routine as a bedtime story every night or as simple as a warm goodbye hug every morning before school. Consistency in your responses also plays a crucial role. If a child knows that their parents will listen calmly to their school day tales, whether joyous or upsetting, they feel secure in sharing their experiences. Predictability in emotional reactions teaches children that no matter what they do or say, the love and support they receive from their parents remains steadfast. This doesn't mean you can't have bad days or moments of frustration, but rather that your overarching demeanor conveys reliability and love.

Creating a safe emotional space is an ongoing process, a commitment to fostering an environment where your child can grow, explore, and express themselves freely. As you implement these strategies, you build more than just a safe space; you weave a resilient, trusting relationship that stands as the foundation of effective co-regulation. This chapter opens the door to understanding how to significantly enhance your child's emotional development and well-being through intentional actions and environments.

2.2 The Role of Empathy in Parenting: Seeing the World Through Your Child's Eyes

Empathy, often envisioned as the ability to walk in someone else's shoes, is a transformative parenting tool that does more than bridge emotional distances; it builds a bridge of deep understanding and connection that is foundational in the parent-child relationship. When you, as a parent, genuinely understand and reflect on your child's feelings, it tells them their experiences and emotions are not only recognized but also valued. This validation is crucial for children as it enhances their self-esteem and improves their emotional and social development.

Think of empathy as the emotional glue that connects you to your child. It involves more than understanding their sadness when they lose a favorite toy or sharing joy at a friend's birthday party. It's about fully appreciating their daily experiences from their unique viewpoint. When your child struggles with a math problem and feels frustrated, empathy lets you genuinely grasp their struggle, not just dismiss it as trivial. This understanding fosters a supportive environment where your child knows they can express their frustrations and seek comfort without judgment. Moreover, empathy strengthens the parent-child bond; it reassures the child that they are not alone in their journey through life's trivial and significant moments. This connection is vital for emotional security and encourages open communication, which is essential for effective co-regulation.

To cultivate this empathetic connection, acknowledge that each child perceives the world differently. This recognition helps you appreciate that what might seem like a minor issue to you can be significant to your child. Regularly engaging in activities you enjoy can provide deeper insight into your child's world. Whether building a model airplane together or drawing in the park, these shared activities offer natural opportunities to observe, engage, and discuss your child's thoughts and feelings. Through these shared moments, empathy naturally develops as you better understand the nuances of your child's personality and emotional responses.

Empathy also plays a crucial role in discipline, a context in which it can sometimes be most challenging to maintain, yet where it is essential. Imagine your child has just drawn on the living room wall. It's easy to react with immediate frustration. However, approaching the situation with empathy involves taking a deep breath and recognizing the incident from your child's perspective. Perhaps they were exploring their creativity or expressing themselves in the only possible way. Addressing the behavior with empathy involves acknowledging their need to express themselves while guiding them toward more appropriate outlets. You might say, "I see you're enjoying drawing. It's important to keep our walls clean, but let's get some paper so you can continue drawing." This approach not only corrects the behavior but also supports your child's emotional needs, thereby maintaining trust and openness in your relationship.

In practicing empathy, perspective-taking is critical. This empathy means striving to see situations through your child's eyes and understanding their feelings without overlaying your judgments or assumptions. One effective way to develop this skill is through reflective listening. When your child speaks, listen carefully, then paraphrase what you think they said and felt. For example, if your child is upset about a friend not sharing a toy, you might reflect, "It sounds like you felt left out when Michael didn't share his toy with you." This technique validates your child's feelings and helps clarify and correct any misunderstandings in perception, ensuring that you see the situation from their perspective.

Another aspect of empathy in parenting is validating your child's feelings. Validation does not mean you agree with every feeling or behavior your child exhibits, but it does mean you acknowledge their feelings as natural and understandable. This validation can profoundly comfort a child; it communicates that their feelings are legitimate and that it's okay to express them. Expressing this validation explicitly is essential, especially in moments of distress. For instance, if your child is scared of the dark, instead of diminishing their fear with a quick dismissal like "There's nothing to be afraid of," try affirming their feeling with a response like, "It can be terrifying when it's dark because it's hard to see what's around. Would you like a nightlight in your room or maybe some company until you feel sleepy?" This response acknowledges their fear and offers comfort and solutions, reinforcing an emotionally safe environment where your child feels understood and supported.

Incorporating empathy into the fabric of daily parenting practices not only enhances the individual well-being of your child but also fortifies the overall family dynamics. It transforms discipline from a battleground into a constructive space where learning and understanding precede punishment and fear. By consistently applying empathy, especially in challenging moments, you teach your child about emotional intelligence and consideration for others and model how they can approach the world with understanding and kindness. As you continue to navigate the complexities of parenting, remember that empathy remains one of your most powerful tools, not just for managing the present but for shaping a compassionate, emotionally aware future for your child.

2.3 Dialogue that Connects: Communication Techniques for Every Age

Effective communication is the linchpin in building and maintaining strong, healthy relationships within your family. It isn't just about talking and listening; it's about understanding and connecting on a deeper level. Every age and stage of your child's development presents unique opportunities and challenges for communication. Tailoring your strategies to meet these developmental milestones enhances clarity and ensures that your message resonates with your child meaningfully. For instance, young children benefit from simple, concrete language and visual aids like gestures or expressive facial expressions, which help them grasp the communicated concept. A more nuanced approach is necessary for teenagers navigating a rollercoaster of emotions and seeking independence. This involves open-ended questions inviting them to express their thoughts and feelings without feeling judged or directed.

Active listening is another critical component of effective communication. This skill requires more than hearing words; it demands engagement with and validation of your child's feelings and perspectives. When you actively listen, you show your child that what they say genuinely matters to you. This practice involves making eye contact, nodding to show understanding, and perhaps most importantly, refraining from interrupting while they are speaking. It also means reflecting on what you've heard to confirm understanding, which can be particularly reassuring for a child. For example, if your child is upset about a disagreement with a friend, you might reflect by saying, "It sounds like you're hurt because you feel your friend didn't listen to your side of the story." Such reflections clarify communication and validate your child's feelings, making them feel respected and loved.

Conflict is inevitable in any relationship, but the way you handle disagreements within your family can significantly influence your child's development and your family's harmony. Teaching practical conflict resolution skills is crucial. This includes encouraging everyone to express their thoughts and feelings openly and respectfully, without fear of retribution or dismissal. Establishing ground rules for disagreements is essential, such as no name-calling, yelling, or interrupting. Teach your child to express their needs or frustrations calmly and clearly, using "I" statements such as, "I feel upset when you borrow my things without asking."

Demonstrate calm and respectful disagreement with your child to show them how conflicts can be resolved peacefully and constructively. Additionally, emphasize the importance of seeking mutual understanding, not just winning an argument. This demonstration might involve finding compromises or agreeing to disagree, which can sometimes be the best resolution.

Encouraging your child to express themselves can be one of the most rewarding parts of parenting. Each child has unique thoughts, feelings, and perspectives, and fostering an environment where they can express these openly contributes significantly to their emotional and psychological well-being. There are many creative ways to encourage expression, particularly for children who struggle to articulate their thoughts verbally. Art, for instance, provides a visual medium through which children can explore and communicate complex emotions. Keeping various art supplies accessible for your child when they feel inspired can be incredibly beneficial. Journaling is another excellent tool, particularly for older children and teenagers. It offers a private space to process feelings or events at their own pace.

Additionally, play remains an essential mode of expression for younger children. Engaging in regular playtime with your child not only aids their emotional and social development but also strengthens your bond with them. Whether through storytelling with their favorite toys or imaginative play scenarios, these activities allow children to explore and express their emotions in a safe and controlled environment.

Nurturing these communication skills within your family lays a foundation for stronger relationships and developing a family culture rich in empathy, understanding, and mutual respect. As your child grows and their world expands, the tools and strategies you've shared will equip them to engage more confidently and competently within the family and the broader world.

2.4 Setting Boundaries with Love: The Balance of Freedom and Limits

In the intricate dance of parenting, setting boundaries plays a pivotal role, much like the banks of a river that guide the flow of water. These boundaries are not just rules or limitations but the frameworks within which children explore, learn, and grow. Clear, consistent boundaries provide a sense of order and safety for healthy emotional development. They help children understand expectations and prepare them to navigate the wider world with a sense of responsibility and respect. Think of boundaries as flexible yet secure safety nets that allow children to explore without fear of falling too far.

Boundaries teach children the consequences of their actions, fostering a natural understanding of cause and effect. For instance, enforcing a basic rule such as "put away toys after playing" instils a sense of organization and fosters respect for personal belongings. When boundaries are clear and consistently applied, children know what to expect. This predictability helps to reduce anxiety as children navigate their daily lives. They understand that certain behaviors lead to specific outcomes, which allows them to make choices that align with the expectations of their environment. This understanding is crucial as they grow and face more complex social situations and moral decisions.

However, setting boundaries is not just about laying down rules; it's also about involving children in the process. This involvement fosters a sense of ownership and responsibility, making them more likely to adhere to these guidelines. Engaging children in discussions about why rules exist and inviting them to suggest their ideas for family rules makes them feel valued and respected. This collaborative approach also helps them understand the purpose behind the boundaries, which deepens their commitment to following them. For example, discussing why a specific bedtime is set helps children comprehend the significance of sleep and how it affects their health and mood. Through such discussions, boundaries become meaningful, and children are more likely to embrace them, even if they occasionally test their limits.

Finding the right balance between freedom and limits is one of the more challenging aspects of setting boundaries. It requires a nuanced understanding of a child's age, maturity, and unique personality. Younger children need more defined boundaries as they have a limited knowledge of safety and consequences. As children grow older and demonstrate increased responsibility and comprehension, the boundaries can be expanded, offering them more freedom. This gradual expansion is critical to fostering independence and confidence. For example, a younger child might hold a parent's hand while crossing the street, but an older child may cross alone once they can safely obey traffic signals and rules. Each step of increased freedom is a building block in their development, reinforcing their ability to handle greater responsibility.

Communicating boundaries with empathy is crucial to ensure they are received positively. When you introduce a new rule or reinforce an existing one, take the time to explain why it's essential. This explanation should be age-appropriate and connect the boundary to important values within your family, such as safety, respect, or kindness. For instance, instead of simply stating, "Don't yell in the house," explain, "We speak calmly and quietly in the house because it shows respect for everyone's need for a peaceful environment." This empathetic approach helps children understand the reasons behind the rules and the values they promote, which enhances their willingness to comply.

Inevitably, children will test boundaries, and responding to such situations with empathy and understanding instead of frustration can make a significant difference between a power struggle and a teachable moment. Acknowledge the child's feelings by reinforcing the boundary "It's time for dinner, and I know you're upset because you want to keep playing," and provide them with a choice or a role in moving forward, "Would you like to come to the table now or in five minutes?" This approach reaffirms the boundary and respects the child's sense of self, promoting a healthy, respectful relationship where both parent and child feel heard and valued.

Boundaries are not just about controlling behavior but guiding children toward autonomy and respect for themselves and others. By setting boundaries with love, involving children in the process, balancing freedom with limits, and communicating with empathy, you lay down the foundational stones for your child's journey toward becoming a responsible, respectful adult. Through these practices, you manage the immediate behaviors and instill values and skills to serve your child for a lifetime.

2.5 From Conflict to Connection: Resolving Emotional Dissonance

Emotional dissonance, a state where one's internal feelings conflict with external expressions, can be particularly challenging in the context of parenting. This dissonance often arises when parents suppress their true feelings to try to maintain a facade of calm or happiness for their children. For example, a parent might hide their frustration or sadness to avoid upsetting their child. However, children are perceptive and can sense when emotions are not congruent, which might confuse them or make them wary of expressing their true feelings. Unresolved emotional tension can build up when there is a gap between what a person feels and what they show, hindering genuine connections. Addressing and resolving this dissonance is crucial, as it strengthens trust and fosters an environment where all family members feel safe expressing their true feelings.

To navigate conflicts constructively, it is essential to equip yourself and your child with practical tools that turn these challenges into opportunities for growth. One effective tool is the 'conflict resolution protocol,' which involves several steps designed to resolve disagreements in a structured manner. Begin by openly acknowledging the conflict and committing to fix it together. Next, each party takes turns to express their perspective using "I" statements, which helps to personalize the feelings without casting blame. For instance, saying, "I feel upset when my suggestions are ignored" instead of "You never listen to me" can make a significant difference. After sharing, both parties should repeat what the other said, ensuring mutual understanding. The final step involves brainstorming solutions, reinforcing teamwork, and showing that collaboration is possible even through conflict.

Rebuilding connections after arguments is another critical aspect of resolving emotional dissonance. It is common for feelings to be hurt after a disagreement, creating a lingering sense of disconnect if not addressed. Strategies for rebuilding these connections emphasize the importance of apologies and forgiveness. Apologizing sincerely, which involves acknowledging the hurt caused and taking responsibility for one's actions, can be a decisive step toward healing. It's equally important to encourage your child to express how the conflict affected them and to listen attentively to their feelings. This open dialogue can lead to a mutual understanding of the emotional impact and help both parties learn from the experience. Integrating a ritual of reconciliation, such as a hug or a special handshake after resolving a conflict, can also help restore emotional connection and reinforce the security of your relationship.

Maintaining connection through disagreements is vital to ensure that conflicts do not permanently damage relationships. It involves respecting each other's viewpoints and emotions, even when they differ significantly from one's own. One way to maintain this connection is through 'emotional holding,' which means acknowledging and validating the other's emotions without immediately trying to change them or offer solutions. This practice allows the child to feel heard and valued, maintaining an emotional connection even when you disagree. Furthermore, setting a positive example by healthily managing your emotions teaches your child to do the same. Demonstrating that disagreements are a natural part of relationships but don't diminish love or respect sets a powerful precedent for your child's future interactions.

Navigating the complexities of emotional dissonance and conflict requires patience, understanding, and active effort. By implementing these strategies, you resolve the immediate issues and build a stronger foundation for your relationship with your child. Each conflict becomes a stepping stone to deeper understanding and a more resilient connection, transforming potential strife into strengthening bonds.

As we conclude this chapter on transforming conflict into connection, we reflect on the journey through the various strategies discussed. From understanding the roots of emotional dissonance to actively engaging in conflict resolution and healing post-disagreement, each step is integral to fostering a nurturing family environment where every member feels understood and valued. These practices involve managing conflicts, enriching familial bonds, and ensuring love and respect prevail even in challenging times. Moving forward, the principles and tools outlined here will guide you in nurturing a home where emotional openness and understanding thrive, setting the stage for continued emotional growth and connection in the subsequent chapters.

Chapter 3:
Navigating Parental Emotions

Imagine you're preparing dinner, the kids are shouting in the next room, and suddenly, the pot boils over. Your heartbeat quickens, your cheeks flush with heat, and a sharp word jumps to the tip of your tongue. It's a moment all parents face, where emotions can quickly spiral out of control. But what if, in that split second, you could tap into a deeper understanding of your emotional triggers, effectively managing your reaction for your peace and your children's well-being? This chapter delves into the complexities of parental emotions, offering you tools and insights to navigate your emotional landscape with grace and understanding.

3.1 Recognizing and Managing Parental Triggers

Identifying Personal Triggers

Recognizing what sets them off is the first step in mastering your emotional responses. Triggers are specific behaviors, words, or situations that prompt a disproportionate emotional reaction within you. For instance, you might be unusually irritated when your child ignores your instructions or deeply hurt when they yell, "I don't love you!" during a tantrum. To identify these triggers, start by maintaining a simple emotion diary. Note incidents that upset you and describe how you felt and reacted. Over time, patterns will emerge, highlighting specific triggers. This practice not only aids in recognizing what affects you but also begins controlling your reactions, as awareness is the first step toward change.

Understanding the Origins of Triggers

Our triggers are often rooted in our experiences, upbringing, or deepest insecurities. Understanding the origins of your emotional triggers can illuminate why certain behaviors from your children affect you so profoundly. For example, if you received frequent criticism as a child, you might be particularly sensitive to your children's criticism or perceived disrespect. This understanding can be emotionally freeing, as it allows you to contextualize your reactions as profoundly personal and not inherently tied to your child's behavior. It's helpful to reflect on your childhood and consider what behaviors or situations made you feel unsafe, unloved, or inadequate. Recognizing these can provide insights into your current sensitivities and offer a pathway to healing old wounds, which is crucial for managing present emotions.

Strategies for Trigger Management

Once you identify and understand your triggers, the next crucial step is managing them. Immediate strategies like mindfulness and grounding techniques can be incredibly effective. Mindfulness involves staying present in the moment and observing your feelings without judgment. A simple mindfulness exercise consists of focusing on your breath and noticing the air entering and leaving your body, which can help center your emotions. Grounding techniques involve connecting with the physical world to detract from emotional escalation. Grounding could be as simple as feeling the ground under your feet or the texture of the fabric of your clothes. These techniques can quickly reset your emotional state, giving you the space to choose a more considered response.

Long-term Trigger Resolution

Addressing the deeper issues behind your triggers often involves therapeutic work, which can lead to significant personal growth and improved relationships. Long-term strategies involve therapy, where a professional can help you explore the roots of your emotional triggers in a structured way. Another powerful approach is reflective journaling, where you explore your triggers and reactions in writing, delving into their origins and contemplating healthier ways to cope. Regular self-care routines can also increase your emotional resilience overall, decreasing the likelihood that your triggers will overwhelm you. This long-term work is crucial, not just for your well-being but for the health of your entire family, as it models healthy emotional management and personal growth.

Navigating your emotional triggers as a parent is not just about preventing adverse reactions; it's about deepening your understanding of yourself, which enriches your relationships with your children. By recognizing, understanding, and managing your triggers and addressing their deeper origins, you set the stage for more genuine, calm, and connected interactions with your children, no matter what challenges arise. This journey of emotional self-awareness can be challenging. Still, it is profoundly rewarding, as each step forward enhances not only your life but also the lives of your children, crafting a legacy of emotional intelligence and mutual respect.

3.2 The Pause Principle: Creating Space Between Stimulus and Response

In the thick of daily parenting, moments arise that test our patience and reactivity, perhaps the spilled milk at breakfast or the bedtime resistance after a long day. In these moments, there is a powerful, transformative technique that can shift the dynamic from potential conflict to calm resolution: the Pause Principle. This approach intentionally creates a brief hiatus between what triggers you and your response. The essence of this principle is simple yet profound: by pausing, you allow yourself the time to choose how to respond rather than react impulsively. This space is where thoughtful parenting blossoms, providing room for more measured, empathetic, and effective interactions with your children.

The benefits of implementing a pause in daily interactions are manifold. Firstly, it helps in preventing the escalation of conflict.

Reactivity tends to breed more reactivity, not just within ourselves but also in our children. A harsh word can lead to a tantrum, and suddenly, a minor issue escalates into a full-blown battle of wills. By pausing, you halt this reactivity cycle, allowing you and your child to cool down. This break can help you approach the situation with a clearer mind and perhaps a different perspective, facilitating a resolution that respects your needs and your child's.

Moreover, pausing can enhance the quality of your interactions. It provides a moment to reflect on your child's underlying needs or emotions, promoting a response more attuned to what they are communicating. Pausing models healthy emotional regulation and deepens your connection with your child, as they feel seen and understood.

Developing the habit of pausing is like any other skill; it requires practice and consistency. One effective technique is the use of deep breathing. When you feel your emotions rising, please take a deep breath, hold it for a few seconds, and then exhale slowly. This simple act can significantly reduce your immediate stress response, giving you a clearer head with which to approach the situation. Another technique is counting, which can be helpful when you feel overwhelmed. Count slowly to ten before responding. This time lets you gather your thoughts and calm emotions, enabling a more considered response. You might also consider using a physical reminder, such as a small stone in your pocket or a bracelet. When you feel triggered, touch this object to remind yourself to pause. This tangible cue can be a powerful tool in reminding you to implement this practice until it becomes a natural part of your parenting approach.

Teaching children the "Pause Principle" is equally beneficial, as it equips them with a crucial skill for managing their emotions and reactions from an early age. Start by explaining the concept to them in simple terms. For younger children, you might say, "Sometimes, we all feel like yelling or crying when things don't go our way. But if we take a moment to stop and take a deep breath, we might think of better ways to solve our problem." Encourage them to practice with you. You can create a 'pause signal' like raising a hand or touching your nose, which anyone in the family can use to signify that they need a moment to collect themselves. Make it a game at first to introduce the concept in a fun way. Over time, as your child sees you consistently applying this principle, they will begin to mirror it. Reinforce their attempts by acknowledging and praising their efforts to pause, especially when they calm down and articulate their needs effectively. This positive reinforcement will motivate them to keep using this technique.

Embedding the Pause Principle into your family's communication repertoire transforms not just individual instances of conflict but the overall emotional landscape of your home. It fosters an environment that values thoughtful reflection over impulsive reactions, and each member feels empowered to manage their emotional responses. This shift enhances the day-to-day interactions and profoundly influences your child's long-term emotional and social development. As you continue to practice and teach this principle, you'll likely find that the spaces between stimulus and response grow richer with understanding, respect, and connection, fundamentally enriching your family's life together.

3.3 Self-Care:
The Non-Negotiable Pillar of Co-Regulation

Self-care often gets sidelined in the hectic parenting routine, where your child's needs can demand all your energy and time. However, maintaining your well-being is not just beneficial for you; it's essential for effective co-regulation with your child. The connection between how well you look after yourself and manage your relationship with your child might not be immediately apparent, but it's profoundly significant. When well-rested, healthy, and emotionally balanced, you're better equipped to respond to your child's needs with patience and empathy. Conversely, when you're exhausted or stressed, your ability to effectively manage your emotions and your child's can be compromised. Think of your well-being as the foundation upon which your parenting rests; if that foundation is shaky, everything else will be too.

A parent's emotional state directly influences the emotional climate of the entire household. Children are incredibly wise and pick up on subtle cues about stress or unrest, even if they don't understand them.

If you're stressed, providing the calm, consistent presence that co-regulation requires is more challenging, leading to a cycle where stress begets more stress within the family environment, affecting everyone's emotional well-being. It's, therefore, crucial to break this cycle by prioritizing self-care and ensuring that you're nurturing your emotional, physical, and mental health. Self-care can be integrated into your daily life through tiny, manageable practices, so you do not need large chunks of free time.

For busy parents, self-care must be practical and adaptable to fit into a packed schedule. Start by identifying small pockets of time dedicated to self-care activities. Even five to ten minutes can be enough for some beneficial practices. For instance, you might start your day with a short meditation or breathing exercises before the children wake up, providing a calm start to the day that can help you maintain a peaceful mindset. Physical care is also crucial; it could be as simple as choosing nutritious snacks or walking around the block. These activities boost your physical health and improve your mood and energy levels, making it easier to handle the demands of parenting.

Creating a sustainable self-care routine requires you to make it a priority consciously. This might mean scheduling specific times for self-care activities just as you would for any other necessary appointment. Communicate the importance of this time to your family, explaining that these moments help you be a better parent. You might also explore activities that can be integrated into family time, such as yoga, where you can invite your children to join you, making it a fun bonding activity while also taking care of your health. Another strategy is to use technology to your advantage; numerous apps are designed to help manage stress and promote well-being, which can be used during short breaks throughout your day.

Modeling self-care for your children is one of the most beneficial aspects of maintaining your health. Children learn by observing the adults in their lives. When they see you taking time for your well-being, they realize that self-care is a normal and essential part of life. This can teach them to value their health and well-being from a young age, setting them up for a healthier approach to life's stresses. Discuss with them why you engage in self-care practices and encourage them to think about ways they can take care of themselves, too. For example, they might have a particular relaxation corner with books and puzzles or join you in simple stretching exercises. By integrating these practices into your family life, you take care of your own health and instill a lifelong appreciation for self-care in your children, enhancing their emotional and physical resilience.

In navigating the complexities of parenting, where numerous demands can pull at your time and energy, self-care is a beacon that reminds us of the need to replenish and restore ourselves not just for our own sake but also for our children's. This chapter underscores the profound interconnection between your well-being and your ability to engage effectively in co-regulation, highlighting practical strategies to integrate self-care into your daily life and the importance of modeling these healthy behaviors to your children. Committing to this essential aspect of parenting ensures you are at your best, equipped to meet the challenges and joys of raising emotionally intelligent, well-adjusted children.

3.4 Seeking Support: Building Your Village

In the tapestry of parenting, each thread represents a different type of support, emotional, practical, or informational, woven together; they strengthen your ability to nurture and educate your children. Recognizing the vital role of a supportive community is akin to acknowledging that parenting was never meant to be a solitary endeavor. The phrase "It takes a village to raise a child" holds profound truth, emphasizing that a network of supportive relationships can significantly ease parenting challenges. This support network is crucial not just for occasional babysitting or practical advice but for providing emotional sustenance and a sense of belonging that can buoy you through the ups and downs of raising children.

Identifying potential sources of support involves looking beyond your immediate circle to the broader community around you. Start with your family and friends, who are often the first line of support. They know you and your children and are typically invested in your well-being. Beyond them, your neighborhood might offer resources like family centers or parenting classes where you can meet other parents in similar stages of life. Schools and pediatricians are also pivotal in the support network, offering professional guidance and connections to other resources. It's also beneficial to consider less traditional sources of support, such as local libraries or community centers, which often host events and workshops that can provide information and new friendships. Additionally, workplaces sometimes offer support through parental leave policies or flexible working arrangements, which can significantly reduce stress for working parents.

Building new support networks can seem daunting, especially if you're new to an area or are naturally more introverted. Joining parenting groups can be a great start. Many communities have organized groups that meet regularly, providing a forum to share experiences, advice, and support. These groups can be found through social media platforms, community bulletin boards, or local community centers. Online communities are also invaluable, especially for parents looking for support outside typical working hours or dealing with more specific issues, such as parenting children with special needs. Websites, blogs, and online forums can connect you with a global community of parents. When joining these groups, whether in-person or online, be proactive. Attend meetings regularly, participate in discussions, and don't hesitate to share your experiences and offer support to others. Over time, these connections can grow into significant pillars of your support system.

Asking for and accepting help is often the most challenging step, primarily due to common barriers such as pride, fear of imposition, or the belief that seeking help is a sign of weakness. It's essential to overcome these barriers and embrace the idea that seeking help is an act of strength, not a weakness. Start small by asking for help with manageable tasks that don't make you feel overly vulnerable, like requesting a friend to pick up your child from school when you're running late. Gradually, as you become more comfortable, you can seek more substantial support. It's also crucial to reciprocate when you can. Supporting others not only strengthens your community bonds but also makes it easier to ask for help when you need it. Remember, accepting help allows others the opportunity to give, which can be as rewarding for them as it is beneficial for you.

Navigating the complexities of parenting requires a robust support system. By recognizing the importance of this support, actively seeking it, and graciously accepting it, you enhance not only your capacity to manage the demands of parenting but also your ability to provide a loving, stable environment for your children. As you continue to build and rely on your village, you'll find that the parenting journey becomes a shared adventure enriched by the contributions and companionship of many.

3.5 From Reactivity to Proactivity: Shifting Your Emotional Patterns

In the fast-paced rhythm of daily parenting, it's easy to find yourself reacting impulsively to your children's actions, especially under stress. This reactivity, quick and unfiltered responses to stimuli, can undermine the calm, nurturing environment you strive to create for your family. Reactivity often stems from stress, fatigue, or unresolved emotions, and it can lead to snap decisions that might not align with your long-term parenting goals. Understanding this emotional reactivity is crucial, as it can significantly impact your ability to co-regulate effectively with your child, affecting the emotional climate of the whole family.

Recognizing your reactive patterns is the first step in transforming your reactivity into proactivity. This involves closely observing your behaviors and noting the situations that typically trigger an automatic response. For instance, you might react sharply when interruptions occur during a busy morning routine or when defiance surfaces over homework tasks. These patterns often form predictably around specific stress points or when feeling particularly vulnerable or overwhelmed. By mapping out these patterns, you become more aware of your emotional landscape and better manage your reactions.

To shift from a reactive to a proactive stance, it's essential to plan. This planning is not about scripting every day in detail, but preparing mentally and emotionally for potential stress points. For example, if mornings are particularly hectic, you might prepare as much as possible the night before or wake up a few minutes earlier to center yourself with a quiet coffee. Anticipating and planning for these moments reduces the likelihood of reactivity because you're equipping yourself with calm and intention ahead of time. Another effective strategy is setting clear, realistic expectations for your children and yourself. This clarity can diminish the chances of frustration arising from misaligned expectations about how a day should progress.

Reflection plays a pivotal role in altering your emotional patterns. This involves taking time to reflect on instances of reactivity and proactivity, assessing what contributed to different responses and the outcomes of each. Keeping a brief journal can be immensely helpful in this process. After a reactive incident, for instance, jot down what triggered you, how you responded, what the outcome was, and how you might handle it differently. This reflective practice deepens your self-awareness and progressively rewires your approach to stressful situations, fostering a more thoughtful, considered response pattern over time.

By understanding and modifying your emotional reactivity and embracing a proactive approach to emotional challenges, you can pave the way for more harmonious and effective interactions with your children. This shift not only benefits your immediate family dynamics but also models crucial emotional management skills for your children, positively influencing their social and emotional development.

This chapter has explored the transformative shift from reactivity to proactivity in parenting. Understanding the nature of emotional reactivity, identifying personal patterns, adopting proactive strategies, and engaging in reflective practices can significantly improve your emotional interactions and co-regulation with your children. This proactive approach not only enhances the emotional well-being of your family but also sets a foundation for your children to develop into emotionally intelligent individuals.

As we close this chapter, we look forward to building upon these strategies. Next, we will focus on extending emotional intelligence beyond the immediate family into schools and communities, reinforcing the pervasive influence of cultivated emotional awareness and regulation in broader societal contexts.

Chapter 4:
Addressing Children's Emotional Challenges

Every parent has witnessed the sudden outburst of tears and screams over what seems like a minor frustration. While often stressful, these moments are not just disturbances to be quelled; they are opportunities for deepening the emotional connection with your child and teaching them how to manage their feelings. This chapter delves into children's emotional challenges, specifically focusing on understanding and managing tantrums, a common yet complex part of child development. By exploring the roots of tantrums and equipping you with practical strategies for managing them, this chapter aims to transform potentially tumultuous experiences into moments of growth and understanding for you and your child.

4.1 The Tantrum Toolkit: Strategies for Calm Co-Regulation

Understanding the Root Causes of Tantrums

Tantrums are not merely episodes of challenging behavior; they are expressions of an underlying emotional turmoil that a child is experiencing and often cannot manage or articulate. Tantrums, commonly occurring in children aged one to four, are part of how young children learn to navigate their emotions and interactions with the world. Developmentally, these years are characterized by rapid growth in physical and cognitive abilities but lag in emotional regulation skills. Children in this age group are beginning to assert their independence and experience desires and preferences more strongly, yet they lack the language skills to express complex feelings effectively. This dissonance between what they need or want and their ability to communicate is often what triggers a tantrum. Factors such as fatigue, hunger, and overstimulation also play significant roles. Recognizing these triggers is crucial, as it helps you preempt potential tantrums by addressing the child's needs before frustrations escalate.

Immediate Strategies for De-escalation

When a tantrum does occur, the immediate goal is to de-escalate the situation gently and effectively. Your calm presence is the most powerful tool at your disposal during these intense moments. First, ensure the child is in a safe environment where they can't hurt themselves or others. Get down to the child's level and use a calm, soft voice to reassure them that you are there. Sometimes, gentle physical contact like a hug or holding their hand can help soothe them, but be mindful to ask if they want to be touched; some children might find physical contact overwhelming when upset. Another effective technique is to use simple, precise phrases that acknowledge their feelings, such as, "I can see you're very upset because you can't have the toy right now." This validation can help decrease the intensity of the emotion. Maintaining a calm environment is also beneficial, reducing sensory input like loud noises or bright lights, which can further agitate an already overwhelmed child.

Long-term Strategies for Reducing Tantrums

To reduce the frequency and intensity of tantrums, focus on building your child's emotional literacy and ability to cope with frustration. Regularly engaging in activities promoting emotional identification and expression can equip your child with the skills to express themselves more effectively. For instance, reading books about feelings and discussing the characters' emotional experiences can enhance a child's vocabulary for their emotions and appropriate ways to express them. Implementing a routine where the child can anticipate regular meals, naps, and playtimes can mitigate triggers like hunger and tiredness. Consistently applying these strategies helps the child feel more secure and understood, gradually decreasing the frequency of tantrums as their emotional regulation skills strengthen.

Co-regulation During and After Tantrums

Co-regulation is not just about managing the tantrum as it happens; it's also about what you do afterward. Once the storm has passed, it's crucial to reconnect with your child through a process of co-regulation. This might involve discussing the event simply, reaffirming your love and support, and guiding them to understand what triggered the outburst. For example, you might say, "It's okay to feel upset when you don't get what you want. Next time, try using words or taking deep breaths to help us feel better." Encouraging them to think about what happened and consider alternative responses helps them develop the skills to manage similar situations in the future. This process teaches essential emotional regulation skills and reinforces the security of your relationship, letting them know that they are loved and supported, no matter how challenging the behavior.

By understanding the multifaceted nature of tantrums and applying these strategies, you can transform challenging moments into valuable teaching opportunities, fostering emotional growth and resilience in your child. As we continue to explore children's emotional challenges, remember that each challenge presents a unique opportunity to strengthen your bond and support your child's emotional development.

4.2 Fear, Anxiety, and the Unknown: Guiding Children Through Emotional Turbulence

Navigating the often choppy waters of a child's fears and anxieties requires a sensitive and informed approach. As a parent, you play a crucial role in helping your child understand and manage their concerns, which can range from the dark to new social situations to more significant worries about change or loss. These fears, while perfectly normal, can significantly impact a child's emotional and mental health if not addressed with care and understanding. Recognizing the signs of fear and anxiety in your child is the first step in this crucial process. These signs can be as overt as crying and clinging, subtle as changes in eating and sleeping habits, or unexplained physical symptoms like stomachaches and headaches, which can often be misinterpreted. Children might not always express their fears verbally, especially if they need to develop emotional vocabulary. They might exhibit increased irritability, restlessness, or a sudden drop in academic performance. Observing changes in behavior, no matter how small, can provide early indicators of anxiety or fear, allowing you to address these emotions before they escalate.

Addressing your child's fears begins with creating a space where they feel safe to express their worries without judgment. This involves active listening and reassuring them that their fears are understood and taken seriously. Using age-appropriate language to discuss their worries is essential, offering explanations that align with their understanding. For instance, if a child is afraid of thunderstorms, explaining the natural causes of storms can help demystify the noise and flashes, reducing fear with understanding. Additionally, introducing coping mechanisms such as deep breathing exercises or creating a 'safe space' in the home where the child can feel secure during moments of anxiety can empower them to manage their reactions. Visual aids like calming jars (glitter jars that the child can shake to watch the glitter settle, mimicking the mind settling) can also be practical tools for younger children to grasp calming down from anxiety visually.

Building a sense of safety and trust is foundational to helping children navigate their fears. This sense of security doesn't come from shielding them from all negative experiences; instead, it develops through consistent, supportive interactions where the child feels they can rely on their parents for comfort and understanding. Regular routines and predictable responses go a long way in building this trust. For example, a bedtime routine that incorporates time for talking about the day can help alleviate the anxiety that has built up and provide a consistent, soothing end. When a child's fear is based on upcoming changes, such as moving to a new school, involving them in preparations and discussing what they can expect can help mitigate the fear of the unknown. The key is to balance acknowledging their fear while reassuring them they have the support and tools to face it.

Empowering children to face their fears does not mean pushing them into fearful situations before they're ready. Instead, it involves gentle, gradual exposure and plenty of support and encouragement. This could look like gradually dimming the nightlight over several nights for a child afraid of the dark or arranging playdates with one child at a time to ease social anxiety. The child's comfort level should determine the pace, making it clear that the objective is to develop confidence and coping mechanisms rather than to eliminate fear. Celebrating small victories is crucial here, as it reinforces the child's ability to manage their concerns and encourages them to keep facing them. This empowerment is an ongoing process, where each small step forward builds resilience and reduces the overwhelming power of fear.

To address these challenges, your role as a parent is less about removing all sources of fear and more about equipping your child with the understanding and tools to navigate their feelings. This not only helps them deal with immediate fears but also builds a framework of emotional resilience that will support them throughout life. As you continue to guide your child through these emotional turbulences, remember that your patience, understanding, and proactive support are invaluable in helping them feel secure and capable in the face of their fears.

4.3 The Loneliness Epidemic: Fostering Connection in a Disconnected World

In today's fast-paced, digitally driven society, loneliness has emerged as a subtle yet pervasive issue, not just among adults but alarmingly among children as well. Unlike adults, who can articulate feelings of isolation, children might display loneliness through less direct means. It's crucial for you, as a parent, to recognize these signs, as they can be significantly different and more nuanced. A lonely child may withdraw from others, show changes in eating and sleeping habits, or even exhibit aggression and irritability. Academic performance might dip, and enthusiasm for previously enjoyed activities may wane. They might also complain of unexplained ailments, which are a physical manifestation of emotional distress. Recognizing these signs early on is the first step in addressing this emotional challenge effectively.

The causes of loneliness in children today often stem from modern lifestyles and technology use. The digital age, while offering connectivity on a global scale, paradoxically breeds isolation as interactions become more screen-based and less face-to-face. Children, even those with active online lives, can feel isolated and disconnected from meaningful human interactions. The allure of screens can also lead to a sedentary lifestyle, reducing opportunities for spontaneous play and interaction with peers in physical settings. Furthermore, the competitive nature of modern schooling and extracurriculars can leave little time for children to nurture true friendships, adding layers of isolation.

To combat loneliness, fostering real connections within the family is foundational. Regular, unplugged family time is vital. Whether through shared meals, games, or outdoor activities, these moments can strengthen familial bonds and provide a solid emotional support base. Encourage open conversations about feelings and experiences. Talking helps gauge your child's emotional state and teaches them to value and seek support through interpersonal connections. Additionally, create an environment that encourages your child to invite friends and provides them with space to interact freely. This helps develop social skills and deepens their relationships with peers, providing a buffer against feelings of loneliness.

The role of community and extracurricular activities in a child's life cannot be overstated in its importance in combating loneliness. These platforms offer more than just skill development; they provide vital socialization opportunities essential for emotional health. Encourage your child to participate in group activities that align with their interests, like sports, music, art, or coding. These activities allow them to connect with peers with similar passions, fostering a sense of belonging and community. It's also important to encourage participation in community service or group projects, which can enhance empathy and a sense of connection to a more significant cause, further alleviating feelings of isolation.

Navigating the challenges of modern childhood requires a proactive approach to fostering deep, meaningful connections. By recognizing the signs of loneliness, understanding its modern-day triggers, and actively cultivating an environment that counters these with robust social interactions within and outside the family, you can help your child build a network of support that guards against the quiet creep of loneliness. As these efforts become part of your routine, they combat current feelings of isolation in your child and equip them with the social skills and networks to face future challenges in an increasingly connected yet isolated world. This proactive approach ensures that your child feels less lonely and values deep human connections in an age where digital interactions are the norm.

4.4 Peer Pressure and Social Stress: Equipping Kids to Navigate Complex Relationships

As children grow, they inevitably encounter the multifaceted world of peer interactions, where the influences of friends and classmates play a pivotal role in shaping behavior, attitudes, and self-perception. Peer pressure, a familiar force within these interactions, can significantly impact a child's behavior and decision-making processes. It's crucial to understand that peer pressure can manifest in various forms, ranging from overt challenges to fit in by engaging in specific activities to subtle shifts in language, attire, or interests to mirror that of their peer group. Children often act against their better judgment or personal preferences out of a strong desire to feel included and valued by their peers. This susceptibility can affect their self-esteem, as children might feel inadequate or undervalued when they perceive themselves as differing from 'the norm' or unable to meet peer expectations. Additionally, decision-making is heavily influenced by peer approval or disapproval, which can lead children to make choices they might not otherwise consider, ranging from trivial matters like fashion to more significant issues involving ethical dilemmas or personal safety.

Fostering resilience is vital to fortifying children against the adverse effects of peer pressure. Building this resilience involves nurturing a strong sense of self in your child, an understanding and appreciation of their values, strengths, and preferences, independent of external validation. Encourage your child to engage in self-reflective activities that help them identify what they truly value and enjoy. This might involve discussions after school about how specific interactions made them feel, or encouraging hobbies and interests that they choose independently of their friends. Developing critical thinking skills is also crucial; teach your child to question why someone is urging them to act a certain way and to consider the consequences of their actions. You can role-play scenarios at home where your child practices saying no or expressing their opinion confidently. This preparation can empower them to make choices that align with their values, even under peer pressure.

Navigating social stress and conflict is another complex aspect of peer interactions. Social anxiety often arises from misunderstandings, competition, jealousy, or the challenges of managing different personalities and preferences. To help your child manage these stresses, ensure they have healthy communication skills. Teach them to express their feelings and needs clearly and respectfully and to listen actively to others. Conflict resolution skills are also vital; guide them on how to find compromise and when to seek adult intervention. Maintaining open lines of communication with your child provides them with a reliable outlet and guidance system as they navigate these challenges. Regularly check in about their social interactions and experiences at school to gauge how they feel and cope with their peer relationships.

Your role in guiding your child's social choices and friendships is delicate and should be approached with a balance of oversight and respect for their autonomy. It's natural to want to protect your child from negative influences, but it's also essential to allow them the space to make their own choices and learn from them. Be proactive in discussing the qualities of healthy friendships, such as mutual respect, trust, and kindness. Share your values and why certain behaviors or traits are important, but also listen to their perspectives and preferences. If you have concerns about a friend or group, express them without ultimatums; explain your reasons and concerns, and encourage your child to think critically about the situation. This guidance helps your child develop the ability to discern who they spend time with and what social norms they accept and perpetuate.

By actively engaging with your child on peer pressure and social stress and providing them with the tools and support to navigate these complex dynamics, you empower them to build healthier relationships and face peer interactions with confidence and integrity. This preparation enhances their current social experiences and lays the groundwork for future relationships in adolescence and beyond. As these discussions and lessons become integral parts of your parenting, they contribute profoundly to your child's social and emotional maturity, preparing them to handle the intricacies of relationships throughout their lives.

4.5 Building Resilience: Preparing Your Child for Emotional Setbacks

Resilience, the ability to bounce back from difficulties and challenges, is as crucial for children as it is for adults, perhaps even more so. As parents, one of your most essential roles is equipping your child to face life's inevitable ups and downs with courage and adaptability. This resilience enables them to cope with current challenges and build the strength and skills they need for future obstacles. Emotional setbacks, whether a minor dispute with a friend or a significant personal loss, can profoundly affect children. However, with your guidance and support, these situations can become powerful lessons in resilience.

Starting with developing problem-solving skills, you can significantly enhance your child's ability to navigate life's challenges. Problem-solving is not just about finding solutions but also about identifying problems, considering possible solutions, and making decisions. Begin by involving your child in daily decision-making processes. For instance, let them choose their outfits, plan weekend activities, or decide the menu for family dinners. Such decisions teach children to weigh options and make choices, fostering independence and confidence. When more significant problems arise, guide them through a structured approach:

- Help them define the problem.
- Brainstorm potential solutions.
- Weigh the pros and cons of each.
- Decide on the best course of action.

After implementing the solution, encourage them to reflect on the process and its outcome, enhancing their ability to handle similar situations. This reflective practice improves their problem-solving skills and deepens their understanding of the consequences of their actions, an essential aspect of developing maturity and responsibility.

Fostering a growth mindset is another pivotal aspect of building resilience. A growth mindset, a concept developed by psychologist Carol Dweck, is the belief that abilities and intelligence can be developed through dedication and hard work. This perspective encourages viewing challenges and failures as opportunities for growth rather than insurmountable obstacles. You can cultivate this mindset in your child by praising their effort and strategies rather than their innate abilities. For example, instead of saying, "You're so smart," emphasize the process they engaged in, and you can say, "I'm proud of how hard you worked on your science project." Encourage them to see challenges as opportunities to learn and grow, and teach them that effort is a path to mastering new skills. When they encounter setbacks, guide them to identify what they learned from the experience and how they can use that knowledge in the future. This approach helps children understand that setbacks are not reflections of their worth but are steps in the learning process.

Celebrating efforts and learning from failure is crucial in reinforcing the lessons that setbacks offer. Recognize and reward efforts, even if they don't always result in success. This recognition shows your child that you value their hard work and dedication, encouraging them to continue putting forth their best effort. When failures occur, shift the focus from disappointment to learning. Discuss what didn't work and why, and explore how these lessons can be applied moving forward. For instance, if a test result could be better, instead of focusing on the grade, discuss what study strategies were used, what was learned, and how preparation can be improved for the next test. This constructive approach prevents discouragement and helps your child see failures as mere bumps in the road, not dead ends.

Building resilience in children prepares them for the challenges they face now and those they will encounter in the future. By teaching them problem-solving skills, fostering a growth mindset, and encouraging them to learn from their successes and failures, you equip them with the tools they need to navigate life's complexities with confidence and poise. As this chapter concludes, remember that each setback your child faces is an opportunity to strengthen their resilience. Your support and guidance are crucial to helping them turn challenges into stepping stones for growth. As we move forward, the focus will shift to how these foundational skills are applied as your child steps into adolescence's increasingly complex social world.

Chapter 5:
Deepening Emotional Connections

Imagine capturing a moment where laughter fills the air, where every giggle serves as a thread weaving stronger bonds within your family. These moments of joy often arise during play, a simple yet profound activity that frequently gets overlooked as children grow older and schedules become busier. Consider this: even the animal kingdom uses play as a critical tool for learning and bonding. If animals instinctively understand the value of play for development and connection, it's worth exploring how this fundamental activity can enhance our families' emotional bonds. This chapter dives into the transformative power of play, revealing how it can strengthen family relationships, synchronizing hearts and minds in a dance of joy and mutual understanding.

5.1 The Power of Play:
Strengthening Bonds Through Shared Joy

Play as a Language of Love

The essence of play transcends mere entertainment; it is a profound language of love that communicates deeply without words. Through play, emotions are expressed and shared, barriers break down, and hearts open. When you play with your child, you enter their world on their terms and show them that you value their interests and enjoy their company. Joining your child's play is a powerful form of validation and love. It affirms to the child that they are worthy of attention and delight. Play also provides a unique opportunity to experience joy together, a cornerstone for a loving and trusting relationship. Shared joy during play creates memories and builds emotional bonds that are carried forward into the child's sense of self and their view of family relationships.

Types of Play for Different Ages

Adapting play to suit your child's developmental stage is a crucial role for parents, ensuring the activity is engaging and beneficial. For toddlers, play is often about exploring the physical world; they revel in sensory play, which involves touching, feeling, and manipulating objects. Engaging in sensory play, such as playing with sand, water, or even simple household items like pots and pans, can provide immense joy and learning opportunities. Imaginative play takes center stage as children grow into preschool and early school years. This form of play allows them to experiment with social roles and scenarios, often mimicking adults. Participating in their imaginative play, whether pretending to be customers at their make-believe store or helping in a superhero quest, boosts their creativity and supports their understanding of social interactions. For older children and adolescents, play might shift towards more structured games with rules, such as board games or team sports. Engaging with them in these activities, learning the rules together, and strategizing can be a thrilling experience that teaches valuable lessons about teamwork and fair play.

Co-regulation through Play

Play is not just about having fun; it is a dynamic tool for emotional co-regulation. When you play with your child, you actively engage in a process where emotions can be shared and managed together. For instance, various emotions can surface during a game, excitement, frustration, disappointment, or joy. These moments provide opportunities for teaching your child how to handle emotions healthily and constructively. If a game doesn't go as your child hoped, you can model how to handle disappointment gracefully or manage excitement without overstimulating. Shared emotional experience during play helps children learn to regulate their emotions and, importantly, understand that they are not alone in their experiences. They realize that emotions, like parts of a game, are transient and manageable and that joy can be found in the process, not just the outcome.

Creating a Play-Friendly Environment

To foster a home environment where play is a central theme, it's up to you, the parent, to create spaces that encourage creativity and spontaneity. An environment that promotes play doesn't necessarily mean having a house filled with toys. Instead, it means having accessible spaces that invite creative engagement. Designate areas in the home where play is encouraged, a corner with art supplies, a space for building blocks or puzzles, or even a backyard for outdoor games. These designated play zones signal to your child that play is an essential and valued activity in the home.

Furthermore, keeping these areas organized and rotating toys or materials can keep the space inviting and engaging for the child. Encourage play by sometimes leaving out a puzzle partially completed or a storybook open, inviting your child to engage. This setup promotes play and subtly teaches organizational skills and respect for shared spaces.

As we explore the myriad ways in which play enhances and deepens emotional connections within the family, remember that the simplicity of play belies its profound impact. Through these joyful interactions, the foundations of trust, empathy, and love are built and reinforced. In the following chapters, we will explore other foundational elements that contribute to deepening emotional connections, ensuring that your family's emotional landscape is one of richness and warmth, where every member feels valued, understood, and connected.

5.2 Mindful Parenting:
The Path to Presence and Connection

Mindful parenting, a term that has garnered attention for its profound impact on family dynamics, is fundamentally about cultivating moment-to-moment awareness of your thoughts, actions, and environment while interacting with your child. This approach encourages you to be present and fully engaged with your child's current experience rather than distracted by past concerns or future anxieties. The benefits of adopting this style of parenting are manifold: it strengthens emotional bonds, enhances communication, and fosters a nurturing environment conducive to open and honest exchanges. Through mindful parenting, you learn to respond to your child's needs and emotions with understanding and empathy rather than reacting based on your immediate feelings or external pressures. This presence helps to create a calm, stable environment where children feel secure and valued, significantly enhancing the emotional connection and promoting effective co-regulation within the family.

Developing mindfulness as a parent involves integrating specific practices into your daily routine that enhance your awareness and presence. One foundational practice is meditation, which can be adapted to fit a busy schedule. A few minutes of seated, quiet reflection daily can significantly increase your mindfulness. During these moments, focus on your breath and observe your thoughts as they come and go without judgment. This practice helps you cultivate a habit of responding thoughtfully rather than reacting impulsively, a skill that directly benefits your interactions with your child. Another practical application of mindfulness involves setting intentional pauses at various points during the day. Before transitioning from one activity to another, take a moment to breathe and become fully present. These pauses are particularly helpful during stress or multitasking, as they allow you to recalibrate and refocus on the present moment and your engagement with your child.

Applying mindfulness in communication with your child transforms ordinary interactions into opportunities for deep connection and understanding. It starts with active listening, where you give your full attention to what your child is saying without planning your response or judgment. Listening reassures your child that their thoughts and feelings are important and valued. When speaking, be conscious of your tone and words, choosing expressions that convey empathy and understanding. For instance, instead of immediately offering solutions or dismissals to your child's concerns, validate their feelings with responses such as, "It sounds like you had a tough day; would you like to talk about it?" This mindful communication fosters a deeper emotional connection, making your child feel heard and supported, essential for healthy emotional development.

Mindfulness also proves invaluable in managing conflicts, both big and small. When tensions rise, a natural and expected part of any family dynamic, mindfulness helps you approach these situations calmly, focusing on finding solutions and maintaining emotional connections rather than winning arguments or correcting behavior immediately. Start by acknowledging your feelings and taking a deep breath to center yourself before responding. Approach the conflict with the intent to understand your child's perspective, asking open-ended questions that encourage them to express their thoughts and feelings. This approach de-escalates potential confrontations and teaches your child how to handle disagreements with composure and respect for others' viewpoints. By consistently applying mindfulness to conflict situations, you create a home environment where collaborative solutions are reached, and each family member feels respected and valued.

Incorporating these mindful practices into your parenting approach invites a shift towards more intentional, aware, and compassionate interactions with your child. As you cultivate mindfulness, you likely notice improvements in your relationship with your child and your emotional well-being. This holistic improvement in family dynamics underscores the transformative power of mindful parenting, making every shared moment with your child more meaningful.

5.3 The Language of Love: Understanding and Speaking Your Child's Love Language

Love languages, a concept popularized by Dr. Gary Chapman, represent how individuals express and experience love. Understanding these can significantly enhance the emotional connections within your family, as it allows you to communicate affection in ways that resonate most profoundly with each member. The five widely recognized love languages are "Words of Affirmation, Acts of Service, Receiving Gifts, Quality Time, and Physical Touch." Each person, including children, tends to express and understand love primarily through one or two of these languages. By identifying and speaking your child's primary love language, you can more effectively convey your love and strengthen your bond, ensuring that your expressions of affection truly fulfill their emotional needs.

Observing your child is the first step in identifying their primary love language. This process requires attention and sensitivity, as children sometimes need to articulate how they prefer receiving love. Instead, look for clues in their behavior and reactions. For example, a child whose love language is "Words of Affirmation" might light up or become more energetic when praised. They may also frequently compliment others, mirroring their preference for receiving love.

On the other hand, a child who thrives on "Quality Time" might frequently request one-on-one activities or express happiness when engaged with them without distractions. A child who responds strongly to "Physical Touch" might often seek hugs or sit close to you, while one who values "Acts of Service" might show appreciation when you help them with tasks or go out of your way to take care of their needs. Finally, a child who cherishes "Receiving Gifts" might treasure even small tokens or become particularly excited about thoughtful and personalized gifts, viewing them as tangible expressions of love.

Expressing love in ways that resonate with your child's love language can deepen your connection. If your child's primary love language is "Words of Affirmation," regularly offer specific and heartfelt praise.

Highlight achievements and character traits you admire, such as kindness or perseverance. For a child who values "Acts of Service," your help with their daily tasks, like setting up a study area or fixing a broken toy, becomes a powerful expression of your love. If your child cherishes "Quality Time," ensure you schedule regular periods where you are fully present with them, engaging in activities they enjoy without distractions from phones or other tasks. For those who feel loved through "Receiving Gifts," consider giving thoughtful presents that align with their interests, and remember, these don't have to be expensive items; even handmade gifts or small surprises can make a significant impact. Lastly, if your child's love language is "Physical Touch," regular hugs, a pat on the back, or a gentle touch on the arm, it can be comforting and reassuring, strengthening the emotional bond between you.

Adapting how you express love as your child grows is crucial, as their needs and perceptions will evolve. What delights a toddler might not hold the same value for a teenager. As children grow, their understanding of and responsiveness to different expressions of love can change. For instance, younger children might primarily appreciate "Physical Touch" and "Words of Affirmation." However, as they enter adolescence, "Acts of Service" and "Quality Time" might become more significant, reflecting their growing desire for independence and deeper emotional interactions. Maintaining an ongoing dialogue about love and affection and encouraging your child to share how they feel most appreciated is essential. This open communication helps ensure that your methods of expressing love evolve with your child's developmental and emotional needs, maintaining a robust and supportive bond through all stages of their growth.

By embracing the concept of love languages and integrating it into your daily interactions, you ensure that your expressions of love are meaningful and impactful and foster an atmosphere of empathy and attentiveness within your family. This understanding allows you to meet your child's emotional needs more precisely, enhancing your relationship and providing them with a secure, affirming foundation from which they can grow and thrive.

5.4 Nurturing Emotional Growth: Encouraging Empathy and Kindness

In the nurturing spaces of our homes, the seeds of empathy and kindness can be planted and cultivated to flourish into behaviors that enhance personal relationships and contribute to a kinder, more understanding world. As parents, you are the primary model from which your children learn to interact with others and perceive emotional cues. When you consistently demonstrate empathy and kindness, you set a powerful example that these are not just preferable ways to interact but are expected and normal. This modeling has a profound impact as children naturally mimic the behaviors they observe in their caregivers. For example, when you express genuine concern for a friend's hardship or show kindness to a stranger, you are teaching your child that these are natural and vital responses to the feelings and experiences of others.

To actively foster empathy and kindness in your children, consider integrating specific activities into your daily routines that encourage these traits. One practical approach is engaging in role-playing games where children can explore various emotional scenarios. For instance, you might use puppets or dolls to enact a situation where one character experiences a setback or disappointment. Have your child guide the characters in offering comfort or assistance. These playful yet meaningful interactions allow children to practice empathy in a safe and controlled environment, helping them understand how to apply it in real-world situations. Another activity could involve encouraging your child to write thank-you notes or messages of appreciation to friends and family members. Appreciation promotes kindness and helps them recognize and express gratitude for the positive actions of others, reinforcing the value of thoughtful communication.

Empathy is crucial in resolving conflicts on the playground, between siblings, or in any other social setting your child navigates. Teaching your child to use empathy in these situations involves guiding them to consider the perspectives and feelings of others involved in the conflict. When a disagreement arises, help your child to pause and reflect on what the other person might be feeling or why they behaved in a certain way. Questions like, "How do you think your sister felt when you took her toy without asking?" or "What do you think your friend needed when he was upset?" help children consider the emotional landscape of the situation. This reflection can lead to more understanding and effective resolutions, as it promotes considering solutions that acknowledge and address the needs of everyone involved, fostering a sense of fairness and care.

Recognizing and celebrating acts of empathy and kindness when you see them in your child's behavior is just as important as correcting them when they stray from these actions. Make a point to acknowledge when your child demonstrates empathy or acts kindly, and be specific about what they did and why it was necessary. For instance, if you notice your child sharing a snack with a friend who forgot theirs, point out the kindness they showed and how it likely made their friend feel included and cared for. These affirmations reinforce that their actions positively impact others, encouraging them to continue behaving in empathetic and kind ways. Additionally, consider creating a family 'kindness chart' where acts of kindness are recorded and celebrated with a family activity at the end of each week, reinforcing the importance of these behaviors through positive family bonding experiences.

By embedding these practices in your daily interactions and routines, you nurture the growth of empathy and kindness in your children and enrich your family's emotional dynamics. These efforts lay a strong foundation for your children to develop into compassionate individuals who value and practice empathy and kindness, enhancing their interpersonal relationships and contributing positively to their communities.

5.5 Celebrating Individuality: Supporting Your Child's Emotional Identity

In the vibrant mosaic of the human experience, each piece, each person, adds unique colors and textures that enhance the overall beauty of the community. Similarly, each child brings their own emotional identity to the family table, a blend of feelings, expressions, and experiences uniquely theirs. Understanding and nurturing this emotional identity is crucial for their overall development. Emotional identity refers to how a child perceives and expresses their emotions, which are shaped by personality, experiences, and the reactions of those around them. This identity influences not only how they view themselves but also how they interact with the world. Recognizing and validating your child's emotional identity affirms their value and supports their journey toward emotional maturity.

Encouraging children to express their unique personalities and emotions is vital to helping them develop a strong sense of self. Giving them the chance to explore their interests and passions without worrying about criticism can encourage this. For instance, if your child is interested in music, providing instruments or arranging lessons can help them express themselves through this medium. Similarly, if they are drawn to art, supplying them with various materials to explore different mediums can be incredibly validating. It's also essential to create an environment where children feel safe to express their emotions verbally, regularly conversing about their feelings and why, especially during significant events or changes, helps them articulate their emotional experiences. Encourage them to describe what happened and how it made them feel, reinforcing the notion that their feelings are important and valid.

Supporting a range of emotional expressions is essential, especially in challenging the often rigid gender stereotypes and cultural norms that can restrict how children are 'supposed' to express themselves. For example, societal norms usually discourage boys from expressing vulnerability or sadness, while girls may be criticized for showing anger or assertiveness. These stereotypes can severely limit a child's emotional identity and expression. As a parent, you can challenge these norms by modeling a broad range of emotional expressions yourself and supporting your child in expressing their emotions fully, regardless of these stereotypes. Validate their feelings by acknowledging them and discussing them without judgment. If your son is sad and needs to cry, assure him that sadness is a natural response and not a sign of weakness. If your daughter expresses anger, help her understand and channel it constructively rather than dismissing it as inappropriate.

Building self-esteem by celebrating individuality is another crucial aspect of supporting your child's emotional identity. When children understand that they are valued for who they are, not just for their achievements or compliance with expectations, they develop a robust sense of self-worth. This can be encouraged by celebrating their unique qualities and contributions. Make a point to notice and commend attributes like kindness, creativity, or thoughtfulness. Celebrate their successes, but emphasize that your love and admiration do not depend on their accomplishments. This unconditional support fosters secure self-esteem, resilience in facing challenges and rejections, inevitable parts of life.

By embracing and nurturing your child's emotional identity, you empower them to be confident and authentic individuals. This support enriches their personal development and enhances the dynamics within your family and the broader community, promoting a culture of acceptance and understanding. As we conclude this exploration of emotional identity, remember that each child is a unique individual with their feelings, thoughts, and perspectives. Celebrating this individuality fosters their emotional growth and contributes to a more diverse, empathetic, and vibrant world.

As this chapter closes, we reflect on nurturing individuality's profound impact on a child's development and self-esteem. By understanding and supporting their emotional identity, encouraging their unique expressions, and building their self-esteem through celebration, we equip them with the confidence to navigate the world authentically. This foundation of self-assuredness and emotional clarity enhances their well-being and enriches their interactions within the community, fostering a more inclusive and empathetic society. The subsequent chapters will continue to build on these themes, further exploring how deep emotional connections and robust personal identities contribute to building resilient, compassionate, and well-rounded individuals.

Chapter 6:
Transforming Family Dynamics

Picture this:

- It's early morning.

- The coffee hasn't kicked in yet.

- Your home is a whirlwind of activity as everyone rushes to start their day.

Amidst the chaos of misplaced shoes, breakfast spills, and the clock ticking down to school and work deadlines, stress levels are peaking, yours and your children's. It's a scenario many families face, one that often seems as unavoidable as the sunrise. However, transforming this daily chaos into harmony isn't just a distant dream; it's a tangible reality that can be achieved through thoughtful strategies and adjustments to your family's routines and communication methods. This chapter delves into practical, effective techniques to convert your home from a battleground of stress into a sanctuary of peace and cooperation.

6.1 From Chaos to Harmony: Strategies for a Peaceful Household

Identifying Sources of Chaos

The first step in transforming family dynamics is pinpointing the sources of chaos and stress within your household. For many families, common culprits include cluttered living spaces, overpacked schedules, and the perpetual balancing act of juggling family members' different needs and activities. Start by observing your family's typical week, "What are the peak stress times? What triggers frustration or arguments? Is clutter contributing to a sense of disorder?" Often, physical clutter in your environment can lead to mental clutter, which escalates stress and discord among family members. By identifying these stress points, you can address them directly and systematically, laying the groundwork for a more organized and peaceful home life.

Establishing Routines for Harmony

Creating structured routines is akin to setting the tempo for a symphony; each note must arrive on time and in harmony with the others to create a beautiful sound. Similarly, well-planned routines bring order and predictability to family life, which can significantly reduce daily stress. This includes consistent wake-up times, mealtimes, homework schedules, and bedtime routines. When everyone knows what to expect and when to expect it, there's less room for chaos and more space for calm. Visual schedules help younger children understand and follow daily routines. For older children and teens, involve them in the planning process, let them have a say in their schedules, which can increase their commitment to maintaining these routines. Regular family meetings to discuss and adjust routines as needed can foster cooperation and ensure everyone's needs are met.

Communication Strategies for Reducing Conflict

Effective communication is the bridge that connects individual family members' needs and desires with the family's overall health. Develop clear, open lines of communication and ensure that every family member feels heard and valued. This involves active listening, paying full attention to the speaker without planning your response, and using "I" statements to express your feelings without blaming others (e.g., "I feel overwhelmed when the living room is cluttered" instead of "You always leave a mess"). Encourage family members to express their needs and frustrations before they escalate into conflicts. Regular check-ins can also be beneficial, providing a dedicated time and space for family members to share their thoughts and feelings about what's working in the family dynamics and what isn't.

Mindfulness and Relaxation Techniques for the Family

Integrating mindfulness and relaxation techniques into your family's routine can transform your home into a haven of peace. These practices help manage stress and foster a sense of calm and presence, benefiting everyone in the household. Consider starting or ending each day with a short family meditation session or practicing deep-breathing exercises together during transition times, such as after coming home from school or work. Yoga can be another effective way for families to engage in mindfulness together. Even simple activities like reading quietly together or listening to calming music can help set a tranquil tone in the home. For families with older children or teens, mindfulness apps can provide guided exercises tailored to different ages and preferences, making integrating these practices into daily life easier.

By addressing these critical areas, identifying sources of chaos, establishing harmonious routines, enhancing communication, and incorporating mindfulness, your family can experience a profound transformation. The shift from chaos to harmony improves the daily logistics of family life and deepens the emotional connections between family members, creating a more supportive, understanding, and loving environment. As you continue to implement and refine these strategies, remember that the goal is not perfection but progress; not absolute peace, but a significant enhancement in how your family navigates the complexities of everyday life together.

6.2 Breaking Generational Cycles: Charting a New Course in Family Dynamics

Every family has threads of behaviors, attitudes, and reactions that weave through generations, often without conscious recognition. These patterns, handed down from parents to children, blend the beneficial and the burdensome. As you navigate the complexities of parenting, recognizing that some of these inherited patterns may not serve your family's current or future happiness is crucial. It begins with keen observation and a willingness to question what you do as a parent and why you do it. Are there aspects of your parenting style that mirror how you were raised, which made you feel undervalued, misunderstood, or unsupported? Identifying these patterns is the first step towards creating a shift that fosters a healthier, more conscious approach to raising your children.

Identifying these generational influences involves reflecting on your childhood experiences and the parenting styles of your parents and their parents before them. Consider the emotions these reflections evoke and whether they influenced your expectations and behaviors towards your children. This reflection can be challenging; it often requires facing uncomfortable truths about people we love and respect. However, understanding these patterns provides a powerful opportunity to choose which to continue and which to change. For example, if you grew up in a household where affection was rarely shown, you might struggle to express warmth and affection naturally. Recognizing this pattern is the first step in consciously embracing and expressing warmth more openly with your children.

Once these patterns are identified, the next step is to break cycles that may be harmful actively. This involves conscious decisions to change specific behaviors and reactions. For instance, if impatience or harsh discipline were part of your upbringing, you may adopt more patient, understanding ways of guiding your children. This doesn't mean the change will be easy or instantaneous. It often requires continuous effort and self-awareness to catch yourself when you fall back into old patterns. Techniques such as mindfulness, where you maintain awareness of your emotions and reactions in the moment, can be beneficial. Additionally, setting intentions daily about how you want to relate to your children can reinforce your commitment to these new patterns. Over time, these conscious choices and efforts can transform not just your behavior but also the emotional landscape of your entire family.

Creating a new family narrative is another transformative aspect of breaking negative generational cycles. This narrative isn't just about rejecting past patterns but about building something new and positive that aligns with your values and your children's needs. It involves crafting a vision of the family dynamics you aspire to, such as one marked by openness, respect, and support. This vision then becomes a guiding principle in your daily interactions and decisions. For example, if a critical part of your new narrative is emotional openness, you might prioritize daily check-ins with each family member to share feelings and experiences. These actions reinforce the new narrative, gradually making it the new norm for your family.

Support systems are vital in sustaining these changes. Breaking entrenched patterns can be challenging; external support can provide encouragement, guidance, and validation. This support can come from various sources, including therapy, parenting classes, and support groups, where you can learn practical strategies and gain insights from others on similar paths. These resources offer practical guidance and remind you that you are not alone in this effort to create a healthier family dynamic. They offer a community and a framework that validates and supports your journey towards positive change.

As you navigate this path of breaking generational cycles and creating a new family narrative, remember that each step forward contributes to a legacy of emotional health and fulfillment for your children. This process transforms your family dynamics and heals and reshapes the emotional blueprint you pass down, offering your children and future generations a foundation of love, understanding, and conscious choice.

6.3 The Family Meeting: A Tool for Democratic Decision-Making

In the bustling rhythm of family life, where decisions range from the mundane to the monumental, family meetings emerge as a beacon of structured communication and collective problem-solving. At its core, a family meeting is more than just a regular gathering; it's a deliberate forum designed to foster open dialogue, ensure everyone's voices are heard, and collectively navigate the family's challenges and decisions. Such meetings are instrumental in teaching children the values of democracy and inclusivity, demonstrating that each family member, regardless of age, has valuable insights and the right to be heard.

The purpose of family meetings extends beyond mere decision-making; these gatherings are pivotal in strengthening family bonds and reinforcing a sense of belonging and mutual respect. They provide a regular, predictable space where family members can express their thoughts, feelings, and concerns, knowing they will be listened to with respect and consideration. This practice enhances family cohesion and instills essential life skills in children, such as articulating their thoughts clearly, listening to others, and contributing constructively to discussions. The benefits are manifold: reduced conflicts, enhanced mutual respect, and a collective approach to problem-solving that can make family challenges less daunting.

Structuring effective family meetings is critical to their success and requires thoughtful organization. Firstly, establish a regular schedule for meetings, whether weekly or bi-weekly, ensuring they are held at a time when all family members can be present without a rush. Begin each meeting with a simple ritual, a moment of silence, or a round of quick gratitude sharing to set a positive tone. Use a talking piece, a simple object passed around, granting the holder the exclusive right to speak. This can help manage interruptions and ensure everyone is heard. Outline the agenda at the start, which can include items brought up by any family member, and encourage an atmosphere where both achievements and concerns can be shared. It's also beneficial to rotate the role of the meeting facilitator, giving each family member, including children, an opportunity to lead. This not only empowers them but also teaches leadership and organizational skills.

Involving children in family meetings from a young age is crucial. It communicates to them that their opinions are valued and that they are integral members of the family unit. Allow them to contribute topics to the agenda and encourage them to express their views on family matters, such as planning for a holiday or discussing weekly meal plans. Younger children might make more straightforward contributions, like choosing activities for family game night or deciding what movie to watch on a family evening. Their ability to engage in more complex discussions will increase as they grow. This involvement helps nurture a sense of responsibility and belonging, which is vital for their emotional and social development. It teaches them how to negotiate, compromise, and stand up for their beliefs in a safe and supportive environment.

Resolving conflicts through family meetings is one of the most significant benefits of this practice. Conflicts inevitably arise within families, but addressing them in the structured, respectful environment of a family meeting can prevent them from escalating and teach constructive conflict resolution. Approach conflicts with a problem-solving attitude, focusing on understanding each person's perspective and finding solutions considering these viewpoints. Encourage family members to express their feelings using "I" statements, which helps reduce blame and fosters understanding. For example, instead of saying, "You never help with house chores," a family member could say, "I feel overwhelmed when I have to do the house chores alone." This approach facilitates a more empathetic dialogue and makes it easier to reach compromises. Additionally, ending meetings with a solution or action plan for each discussed issue not only resolves conflicts but also instills a sense of accomplishment and collective responsibility.

Regularly engaging in family meetings cultivates a family culture where democracy, respect, and open communication are the norm. This culture enhances the day-to-day harmony of family life. It equips children with interpersonal skills that will serve them well beyond the home, in friendships, future workplaces, and their adult relationships. As you continue to refine and adapt the structure of your family meetings to the evolving needs of your family members, remember that the ultimate goal is to foster an environment where each person feels valued, understood, and actively part of the family's journey. Through this ongoing practice, you're not just making decisions about what's for dinner or where to vacation; you're strengthening the foundational bonds of your family and building a legacy of inclusivity and mutual respect.

6.4 Cultivating a Culture of Gratitude and Appreciation

In the tapestry of family life, gratitude and appreciation weave patterns that strengthen the fabric of relationships, enhancing the overall warmth and resilience of family dynamics. Cultivating a culture of gratitude within your family can fundamentally transform the atmosphere of your home, turning everyday interactions into moments of meaningful connection and deep appreciation. Gratitude, in its essence, shifts the focus from what is lacking to what is abundant, from frustrations to blessings, fostering a shared sense of contentment and positivity among family members. This shift enriches your family's emotional environment and equips each member with a more appreciative and resilient perspective toward life's inevitable challenges.

The impact of fostering a culture of gratitude extends far beyond mere pleasantries. When family members regularly express gratitude to one another, it reinforces positive behaviors and deepens emotional bonds. This practice helps each person feel valued and acknowledged for their contributions, big or small, which boosts self-esteem and encourages ongoing positive contributions to family life. Moreover, gratitude enhances empathy, as regularly recognizing the good in others helps them see things from their perspective and appreciate their efforts and challenges. This empathetic connection reduces conflicts and misunderstandings, as appreciation becomes the lens through which family members view one another.

Implementing daily practices of gratitude can be simple yet profoundly effective. One engaging method is maintaining a family gratitude journal. Place a journal in a common area of your home, perhaps on the kitchen table or in the living room, where family members can jot down things they are grateful for throughout the day. These can range from significant events to simple pleasures, like a delicious meal, help with homework, or a fun family game night. Regularly, perhaps during dinner or before bedtime, encourage each person to share something they wrote in the journal. This practice promotes gratitude and provides insight into what each family member values, strengthening connections and understanding within the family.

Another practical approach is the 'gratitude jar,' where family members can drop notes of gratitude, which can be read together at the end of the week or month. This can become a cherished ritual that everyone looks forward to, providing tangible proof of the family's blessings and shared moments of joy. Additionally, integrating expressions of gratitude into everyday conversations is a powerful way to cultivate an appreciative mindset. Simple phrases like "Thank you for helping with the dishes, I appreciate your help," or "I'm grateful for your humor;

you always know how to make me smile" can make a big difference in the overall tone of family interactions.

Recognizing and appreciating each family member's efforts and contributions is crucial in nurturing an environment where everyone feels valued and understood. Make it a point to acknowledge the successes and efforts, regardless of the outcome. For instance, if a child has worked hard on a school project but didn't get the grade they hoped for, focus on their dedication and perseverance rather than the grade itself. Celebrate the effort and the learning process, reinforcing that their value doesn't hinge on perfect outcomes but on the integrity and effort they bring into their endeavors.

Gratitude can also be a transformative response to challenges and setbacks. Adopting a gratitude mindset helps reframe difficulties as opportunities for growth and learning. When a challenge arises, encourage family members to identify aspects of the situation for which they can be grateful. For instance, after a difficult day, you might discuss what you learned from the experience or how it brought the family together to support each other. This perspective doesn't negate the difficulties but offers a way to navigate them with a more resilient and hopeful outlook.

By embedding these practices of gratitude and appreciation into the fabric of your family life, you create a nurturing environment that celebrates each member's worth and contributions, fostering a collective resilience and positivity that can weather both everyday stresses and more significant challenges. As these practices become a natural part of family interactions, they enhance the quality of relationships and equip each family member with a profound appreciation for life's gifts, enriching their interactions beyond the family and into every area of their lives.

6.5 Designing Family Rituals: Creating a Sense of Belonging and Identity

Family rituals, those repeated actions and traditions uniquely tailored to each family, profoundly shape a family's collective identity and foster a deep sense of belonging among its members. These rituals, from daily habits to annual celebrations, are the threads that weave the fabric of family life, imbuing it with meaning, continuity, and a sense of heritage. They act as anchors, providing stability and comfort, and as a reminder of shared values and histories. In our fast-paced world, where external commitments constantly pull individuals in different directions, these rituals bring everyone back together, ensuring that the family remains at its core amidst the chaos of everyday life.

Creating meaningful rituals that reflect your family's values, traditions, and interests begins with an introspective look at what is most important to you and your loved ones. It involves identifying activities that are special to your family or can be imbued with new meaning. For instance, consider a regular family game night where everyone disconnects from digital devices to engage in board games, fostering teamwork and healthy competition. Alternatively, a weekly' family council' where each member shares their highs and lows of the week can become a ritual that encourages open communication and mutual support. The key is to select rituals that resonate with your family's unique ethos and can be realistically integrated into your daily or weekly routines. These rituals should not feel like another task on the to-do list; instead, they should be moments everyone looks forward to, times when memories are made and bonds are strengthened.

Adapting these rituals as your family grows and evolves is crucial. What works for a family with young children may hold different appeals or feasibility for teenagers. As children grow, their interests, schedules, and social lives develop, necessitating a shift in family rituals to accommodate these changes. This adaptation might mean altering the times and days of these rituals or the activities themselves to maintain engagement and relevance. For example, transitioning from storytime with young children to a book club format with adolescents can preserve the ritual of reading together while respecting your children's growing independence and maturation. The flexibility to evolve these rituals keeps them alive and integral to the family fabric, ensuring they continue to foster connections and not become obsolete practices.

Moreover, rituals for connection and celebration play a significant role in marking milestones and reinforcing family unity. Celebrating birthdays, anniversaries, and achievements becomes a way to honor each family member's journey and their part in the larger family story.

These celebrations can be as simple as a special meal cooked together at home or as elaborate as a surprise party. The celebration itself, irrespective of scale, is vital; it acknowledges and shows appreciation for each family member, strengthening emotional bonds. Seasonal rituals, such as decorating your home together for the holidays or planning a family outing at the start of spring, also offer opportunities to cultivate traditions that can be passed down through generations, enriching your family's legacy.

As you weave these rituals into the fabric of your daily life, they become more than just activities; they evolve into cherished traditions that reinforce your family's values, celebrate its joys, and provide comfort during its challenges. These rituals serve as a powerful testament to the unity and identity of your family, reinforcing a sense of belonging and togetherness that nurtures each member's sense of self within the collective family narrative.

As we conclude this exploration of family rituals, we see how they are not just schedules on a calendar but are the heartbeats of familial life. They fortify bonds, celebrate individuality within the family framework, and create a reservoir of shared memories that hold the power to comfort, connect, and guide through generations. Moving forward, the focus will shift to daily interactions and the subtle yet impactful ways they shape the emotional climate of family life, continuing our journey towards nurturing a loving and resilient family environment.

Chapter 7:
Everyday Co-Regulation

Imagine the serene silence of early morning, just as dawn breaks, when the world feels fresh and new possibilities seem to whisper in the cool air. Now, picture your home during these early hours, instead of chaos and the mad dash associated with morning routines, there exists a calm and collected start, setting a positive tone for the day ahead. Often fraught with hurry and stress, Mornings hold a golden opportunity for co-regulation between you and your children. When approached with intention and strategy, these first hours can transform from a time of stress to a moment of connection and emotional alignment, laying the groundwork for a day filled with more understanding and less conflict.

7.1 Morning Routines Without the Rush: Starting the Day on a Positive Note

Establishing a Calm Morning Routine

The tone of your morning often sets the pace for the entire day, not just for you but for your children as well. A calm start can significantly influence the emotional climate of your household, encouraging a sense of peace and readiness to face the day's challenges. This calmness is especially crucial for children whose emotional barometers are highly sensitive to the environment. By establishing a morning routine that prioritizes tranquility, you provide your children with a model of how to manage their mornings peacefully, which can influence their ability to regulate their emotions throughout the day.

One effective way to cultivate a serene morning is to rise before the rest of the household. This quiet time allows you to center yourself and prepare mentally and emotionally before diving into the day's demands. During these moments, engage in a practice that grounds you, meditation, a short yoga session, or simply enjoying a cup of coffee in silence. This personal calmness will make you more available and present for your children, enabling you to meet their morning energy with patience and grace.

Strategies to Avoid Morning Stress

Proactive planning is critical to reducing morning stress. One practical strategy is to prepare as much as possible the night before. Lay out clothes, pack lunches, and set out breakfast items. Involve your children in these preparations to lighten your load and teach them valuable organizational skills. Creating a visual schedule for younger children can help them understand the morning flow and engage cooperatively. This schedule could include simple images representing activities such as brushing teeth, getting dressed, and eating breakfast, providing a clear and engaging guideline for them to follow.

Anticipate potential stress points and plan alternatives. If mornings are hectic due to everyone getting ready simultaneously, consider adjusting wake-up times in increments of fifteen minutes. This staggering allows individual attention to each child and reduces the bathroom or kitchen congestion that often escalates morning tensions.

Incorporating Co-Regulation into Morning Tasks

Morning tasks offer excellent opportunities for co-regulation. Simple activities like choosing what to wear or helping to prepare breakfast can become collaborative efforts that not only get the job done but also strengthen your emotional connection. For instance, when deciding on clothes, present two appropriate options and let your child choose one. This choice fosters independence while keeping the routine efficient. Similarly, involve your child in breakfast preparation; tasks like setting the table or stirring the pancake batter are helpful and give a sense of responsibility and accomplishment.

These shared tasks should be approached with dialogue that encourages emotional expression. For example, as you prepare breakfast, you might discuss the day ahead, sharing any worries or exciting events. This communication demonstrates that you value their input and feelings, reinforcing the emotional support system vital for effective co-regulation.

Mindful Mornings

Incorporating mindfulness into your morning routine can significantly enhance emotional connections and well-being. Mindfulness involves being fully present in the moment and aware of your and your child's feelings and surroundings without judgment. Start by integrating simple mindfulness exercises into your morning routine. This could be as brief as taking three deep breaths together before breakfast to center yourselves or practicing a short gratitude exercise, where each family member states one thing they are grateful for. These practices set a reflective and appreciative tone for the day, modeling emotional regulation and conscious presence.

Consider a mindfulness reminder in a visible place, such as a note on the fridge or a sticker on the bathroom mirror. This visual cue prompts you and your children to pause and breathe deeply. It is a gentle reminder to engage in mindfulness throughout the day, enhancing emotional regulation and connection.

By transforming your mornings from rushed to regulated, you ensure a smoother start to the day and cultivate an environment where emotional intelligence is nurtured. These morning practices lay a calm foundation, preparing you and your children to handle the day's challenges with greater emotional resilience and connectivity. As these morning routines become ingrained, they enhance daily interactions and contribute to a lifelong skill set for emotional management and meaningful relationships.

7.2 Homework and Co-Regulation: Turning Struggles into Opportunities for Connection

The time allocated for homework is often fraught with potential stress for you and your children. This daily routine can bring about frustration, anxiety, and sometimes even tears, not only disrupting the emotional calm of your household but also impacting your ability to connect positively with your child. Understanding the common emotional triggers that arise during homework time is crucial. These can range from a child's fear of failure and frustration over complex tasks to a parent's impatience for tasks to be completed or concern over academic performance. Recognizing these triggers as natural responses to learning challenges helps reframe these moments as opportunities for teaching valuable emotional regulation and problem-solving skills.

Creating a collaborative homework environment starts with setting up a space conducive to learning. This means a quiet, well-lit area consistently designated for homework, free from television and household commotion distractions. In this space, ensure all necessary supplies are at hand to avoid the disruption of searching for items mid-homework. The physical setup should invite focus and calm, including elements your child finds comforting or motivating, such as a favorite piece of art or a plant.

Breaking homework tasks into manageable parts is another strategy that can lessen homework stress. This approach makes the work seem less daunting to your child and allows for easier progress monitoring, which can be encouraging for both of you. Guide your child in planning their homework by discussing what needs to be done and estimating how much time each part will take. You can use a timer to manage these increments, which helps maintain focus. Throughout, keep your communication open and supportive, emphasizing effort over perfection. Praise their progress sincerely and frequently, focusing on their dedication and resilience rather than the correctness of their answers.

Moreover, homework time offers a prime opportunity for you to model the self-regulation skills of patience and perseverance. Demonstrating calm and composed behavior in the face of homework challenges teaches your child how to handle academic stress constructively. Suppose a particular problem is causing frustration; model problem-solving by discussing how to approach the task differently, or suggest taking a brief break to clear the mind. Your approach to these challenges not only teaches academic skills but also imparts life lessons in managing stress and emotions.

Conflicts during homework time are not uncommon and can arise from various sources, such as a child's resistance to starting homework, struggles with specific assignments, or tensions from a long school day. Rather than viewing these conflicts as unfavorable, treat them as opportunities to teach your child about conflict resolution and emotional self-management. Engage your child in a conversation about what is making the homework difficult. Listen to their concerns without interrupting, and validate their feelings. This acknowledgment often alleviates a significant part of the stress. Then, work together to find solutions. Agree on a short break or a change of subject before returning to a challenging task, or discuss strategies for asking for help from teachers.

By viewing homework time through the lens of co-regulation, you transform these daily challenges into valuable teaching moments. This approach enhances your child's learning experience and strengthens your relationship, building a foundation of mutual trust and support beyond academic success. As you consistently apply these strategies, you not only ease the homework routine but also foster an environment where learning and emotional growth progress hand in hand, preparing your child not just for school but for life's various challenges.

7.3 Digital Dilemmas: Navigating Screen Time with Emotional Intelligence

In today's digital age, screen time is an unavoidable part of daily life for adults and children. While digital devices can offer educational content and a way to stay connected with friends and family, managing screen time presents unique challenges. The impact of excessive screen use is multifaceted, affecting emotional and physical well-being. It can lead to reduced physical activity, disrupted sleep patterns, and even impede the ability to recognize and process emotions effectively when face-to-face interactions are replaced by screen-based communication. Understanding how to balance screen time within your family is crucial in fostering a healthy environment where digital tools enhance rather than detract from your family's well-being.

Balancing screen time effectively requires a thoughtful approach that considers screen use quantity and quality. Engaging with your children about what they are watching or playing is as important as monitoring how long they are doing it. To initiate this balance, start by setting clear, age-appropriate screen time guidelines and considering each child's needs. For instance, younger children benefit from stricter limits and more curated content. In comparison, older children might have more flexibility but with agreed-upon restrictions to ensure that screen use does not interfere with sleep, homework, or physical activity.

Setting these boundaries empathetically is critical to ensuring they are adhered to without conflict. Involve your children in decision-making to give them a sense of ownership over their media consumption. This can be done during a family meeting where everyone discusses and agrees on screen time limits, acceptable content, and even 'technology-free' times or zones within the house. When children understand the reasons behind these rules and participate in creating them, they are more likely to follow them. Explain the benefits of these boundaries, such as having more time for family activities or outdoor play, which can help them perceive these rules positively.

Co-regulation during screen time is another strategy that turns a typically solitary activity into an interactive and relational experience. This could involve watching a show together, discussing the storyline, character motivations, and behaviors, or playing a video game with your child and navigating challenges together. These shared activities allow you to understand the content's impact on your child and provide opportunities to discuss emerging themes or issues. It also helps you model appropriate responses to content, such as handling winning or losing in games or thinking critically about media messages. By co-viewing, you make screen time a cooperative, learning, and bonding experience rather than a passive activity.

Teaching self-regulation in the digital world is crucial for helping children manage their screen time as they age. Techniques for self-regulation can be modeled by setting personal examples, such as avoiding screens during meals or turning off devices well before bedtime. Encourage activities that don't involve screens and are enriching or physically engaging, such as reading, playing sports, or creative arts. Discuss the feelings and urges when it's time to turn off the device and strategies to handle those emotions, such as taking deep breaths, discussing what was enjoyable about the screen time, or planning a preferred activity to transition to afterward.

By addressing digital dilemmas with emotional intelligence, you equip your children with the skills to navigate their digital worlds in a balanced and emotionally aware manner. This enhances their ability to engage with digital media critically and ensures that their overall development remains holistic and grounded in real-world interactions and experiences. As you implement these strategies, the dynamic of screen time in your home can shift from a potential source of conflict to an opportunity for growth, learning, and connection.

7.4 Mealtime Moments: Fostering Connection Over Food

Gathering around the dining table, where plates clink gently against the hum of shared stories and laughter, is more than a time to refuel. It's a cherished ritual that knits the fabric of family life, threading each day with moments of connection and mutual understanding. Shared mealtimes are a cornerstone for nurturing family relationships and offer a consistent opportunity for emotional co-regulation. During these gatherings, each family member can slow down, engage, and tune into one another's emotional states, making it an ideal setting to strengthen bonds and enhance family dynamics. Eating together, discussing various topics, and sharing the highs and lows of the day encourages a rhythm of interaction that is both nurturing and grounding. This regular congregation at the meal table helps create a predictable structure that children find reassuring, knowing there is a dedicated time and space to share their thoughts and feel heard.

Involving children in meal preparation can transform cooking from a chore into a joyful and educational activity that enhances family cohesion. Engaging children in the kitchen does more than lighten your workload; it teaches valuable life skills and fosters a sense of responsibility and accomplishment. Start by inviting them to participate in age-appropriate tasks such as washing vegetables, stirring batter, or setting the table. Snapping green beans or tearing lettuce can make younger children feel involved and valuable. Older children and teenagers can take on more complex tasks like measuring ingredients, following a recipe, or planning and cooking a small dish. As you cook together, narrate what you're doing and why, explaining how different ingredients and techniques create a meal. This educates them about food and cooking and opens up a space for casual conversation, allowing children to talk about things on their minds in a relaxed setting.

The conversations that unfold over meal preparation and dining are invaluable. This is an opportune time to discuss the day's events, share feelings, and address any challenges that might have arisen. Encourage each family member to discuss their day, highlighting positive experiences and difficulties. Use open-ended questions to facilitate deeper discussion and show genuine interest in their responses. For example, ask, "What was something interesting that happened today?" or "How did you feel about that test/project/meeting?" Such questions prompt sharing and help children and adults reflect on their experiences and emotions, fostering emotional intelligence and resilience. Sharing and listening enhance empathy among family members, as each person gains insight into the others' daily lives and emotional landscapes.

Mindful eating practices integrated into family mealtimes can significantly enhance the quality of these interactions by encouraging presence and attentiveness. Mindful eating involves paying full attention to the experience of eating and drinking, both inside and outside the body. Teach your family to notice the food's colors, smells, textures, and flavors, appreciating each aspect. Discuss the origins of the food and the effort that went into preparing it, and express gratitude for having food on the table. This approach enriches the eating experience and teaches gratitude and appreciation for the simple pleasures in life.

Additionally, practice eating slowly and without distractions like television or smartphones. This improves digestion and ensures that mealtime is dedicated to family interactions. Encourage conversations about the sensory aspects of the meal, which can be particularly engaging for children as they learn to articulate their experiences and preferences.

By centering family life around nourishing interactions at mealtimes, you cultivate a routine reinforcing the importance of togetherness, communication, and mutual care. These mealtime moments become more than just about food; they are pivotal daily touchpoints that strengthen family bonds, teach valuable life skills, and foster an environment where every member feels valued, understood, and emotionally connected. Through these practices, you feed the body and nourish the heart and soul of your family, ensuring that the simple act of eating together becomes a cherished pillar of family life.

7.5 Bedtime Rituals: Ending the Day with Emotional Closeness

As dusk settles and the world quiets, bedtime emerges as a sacred time for families to wind down the day's activities and prepare for a restful sleep. This transition from day to night is not just about physical rest but is also a crucial period for emotional connection and reassurance. Establishing a calming bedtime routine is vital to signal the end of the day, set the stage for peaceful sleep, and strengthen the emotional bonds between you and your child.

A calming bedtime routine begins with predictable, soothing activities that signal to your child's body and mind that it's time to slow down. This might include dimming the lights, which helps stimulate the production of melatonin, the sleep hormone, or playing soft, soothing music that fills the room with tranquility. Engaging in quiet activities like reading a book together or doing some gentle stretches helps ease the transition from the busyness of the day to the calm of the evening. During these activities, maintain a soft and soothing tone of voice and encourage your child to move slowly and calmly. These consistently practiced signals become cues that help your child recognize and adapt to bedtime, making the process smoother and more enjoyable for both of you.

Bedtime also offers a precious opportunity for emotional connection. This can be beautifully facilitated through bedtime stories, a practice that does more than entertain; it opens doors to new worlds and ideas and invites sharing and discussion. Choose books that interest your child and spark emotions and ideas. Discuss the characters' decisions and feelings, drawing parallels to real-life situations. This enhances your child's empathy and understanding and allows the sharing of personal experiences and emotions. Alternatively, share the highs and lows of your day with your child and encourage them to do the same. This practice fosters open communication, allowing your child to go to bed feeling heard and understood. For younger children or those less inclined to talk, cuddling can be a powerful way to connect. The physical closeness, the warmth, and the heartbeat rhythm provide comfort and security, speaking volumes even without words.

Addressing bedtime fears and anxieties is another critical aspect of nighttime routines. Many children experience fears that manifest more intensely at night, whether it's fear of the dark, nightmares, or separation anxiety. It's essential to approach these fears with validation and reassurance, not dismissal. Acknowledge your child's fear as genuine and reasonable, and discuss it openly. Offer comfort through your presence, letting your child know they are not alone. You can introduce nightlights or "monster sprays" made of water and essential oils to empower them to manage their fears.

Additionally, practicing relaxation techniques like deep breathing or guided imagery can be very effective. Teach your child to breathe deeply through their nose, hold for a few seconds, and then exhale slowly through their mouth, imagining their fears leaving their body with each breath. Such techniques help alleviate immediate anxiety and equip your child with tools they can use independently.

Incorporating relaxation techniques into the bedtime routine can significantly enhance the quality of sleep and the emotional connection between you and your child. Techniques such as progressive muscle relaxation, where you guide your child to tense and then relax different muscle groups, help release physical tension and mental stress. You can make this practice more engaging by incorporating storytelling, such as imagining a journey where each relaxed muscle helps them float gently to a dreamy sleep. Meditation apps designed for children can also offer guided relaxations that are both fun and calming. These practices help your child unwind and provide a shared ritual that deepens trust and security, reinforcing your bond.

As this chapter concludes, the essence of bedtime rituals as a cornerstone of daily co-regulation becomes clear. These nightly practices do more than prepare your child for sleep; they weave a tapestry of security, understanding, and connection that supports emotional and physical health. They transform bedtime into a cherished ritual for healing and bonding, ensuring your child drifts into sleep feeling safe, loved, and connected. As we progress, the focus will shift to exploring how these foundational practices can be extended beyond the immediate family setting, enhancing your child's ability to navigate the broader world with emotional intelligence and resilience.

Chapter 8:
Overcoming Obstacles to
Co-Regulation

Imagine a scenario all too common in parents' lives: a disagreement arises over handling a child's emotional outburst. One parent thinks a gentle, reassuring approach is best, while the other believes in a firmer stance. The air thickens with tension, not just between the child and the parents but also between the parents themselves. It's a delicate dance, balancing personal beliefs with collective goals, all under the watchful eyes of young, impressionable minds. This chapter delves into the heart of such challenges, exploring how to navigate parental disagreements, align co-regulation strategies, and maintain a united front, all while keeping the family's emotional health at the forefront.

8.1 When Parents Disagree:
Finding Common Ground in Co-Regulation
Strategies

Navigating Parental Disagreements

The importance of finding common ground on co-regulation strategies cannot be overstated. When parents present conflicting approaches to handling emotions, it can create confusion and insecurity in children, who thrive on consistency and predictability. The first step in navigating these disagreements is acknowledging that different parenting styles are often rooted in each individual's upbringing and personal experiences. Recognizing this can foster empathy between partners, as each understands that the other's parenting choices are not arbitrary but are informed by deeply ingrained beliefs and experiences.

To effectively navigate these waters, start by identifying your core values regarding child-rearing. What are the non-negotiables for each of you? What outcomes are you both committed to achieving? Often, you'll find that the end goals, raising happy, healthy, emotionally intelligent children, are shared, even if your methods differ. With these common goals in mind, discussions about specific strategies become less about winning an argument and more about finding the best path forward.

Communication Strategies for Parents

Effective communication is the linchpin in aligning co-regulation approaches. It involves transparent, honest, and respectful conversations where both parties feel heard and valued. Begin by setting aside uninterrupted time to discuss your parenting strategies, perhaps after the children have gone to bed or when you're both relaxed and undistracted. Use "I" statements to express your feelings about specific approaches, such as, "I feel worried when we raise our voices because it might scare the kids and close them off." This technique minimizes defensiveness and focuses on personal feelings rather than accusations.

Active listening is equally crucial. This means hearing your partner, not planning your following counterpoint while they speak. Reflect on what you hear to ensure understanding, and ask open-ended questions to delve deeper into each other's perspectives. Through these respectful exchanges, you can start to weave together a cohesive parenting tapestry that incorporates the best of both worlds, tailored to the unique needs of your children.

Working Together as a Team

Emphasizing teamwork in your co-regulation strategies can transform potential conflicts into opportunities for strengthening family bonds. Discuss each parent's strengths and how these can be leveraged in managing children's emotional challenges. For instance, if one parent is particularly good at de-escalating conflicts, they might take the lead in tense situations while the other offers support and reinforcement. By working as a team, you model healthy relationship dynamics for your children and create a family environment where each member's strengths are recognized and valued.

Setting up regular family meetings can also be beneficial. These meetings provide a platform for discussing what's working and what isn't, allowing for continuous refinement of your co-regulation strategies. They also give children a voice in family dynamics, helping them feel respected and part of the team. This inclusive approach fosters a sense of unity and shared purpose, reinforcing the family's commitment to supporting one another emotionally.

Seeking External Support if Needed

Sometimes, despite best efforts, finding common ground on co-regulation strategies can be challenging. In such cases, seeking external support can be invaluable. Family counseling provides a neutral space to explore different parenting styles and their impacts under the guidance of a professional. A counselor can offer fresh perspectives and mediation, helping to break through impasses and develop effective co-regulation strategies that respect both parents' views while prioritizing the children's emotional well-being.

Engaging in parenting workshops or seminars together can also be beneficial. These educational opportunities allow parents to learn about child development and effective emotional regulation strategies from experts. This shared learning experience can unify your parenting approach and provide new tools and techniques for managing family dynamics more harmoniously.

By embracing these strategies, you can navigate the complex terrain of parental disagreements gracefully and effectively, ensuring that your home remains a sanctuary of emotional support and understanding. This approach not only resolves immediate conflicts but also sets a foundation for long-term emotional health and resilience within the family, demonstrating the profound impact of united parenting in fostering an environment where children and parents alike can thrive emotionally.

8.2 The Solo Parent Challenge: Co-Regulating Without a Partner

Parenting, even under the best of circumstances, presents a kaleidoscope of challenges and rewards. For solo parents, these challenges often magnify as they navigate the dual roles of nurturing and discipline without a partner. This unique parenting dynamic necessitates a tailored approach to co-regulation, where emotional attunement and clear, consistent communication with your child become your primary tools for fostering a stable, loving environment.

Unique Challenges for Solo Parents

The solo parent often faces the steep task of being the sole emotional anchor for their child while also managing the household and possibly juggling work. This multifaceted responsibility can lead to emotional and physical exhaustion, making it difficult to maintain one's emotional equilibrium, let alone help regulate a child's emotions. Recognizing this, it's important first to acknowledge the breadth of your role and the strength it requires. This acknowledgment isn't just about giving yourself credit; it's about recognizing that feeling overwhelmed is not a sign of weakness but a predictable response to your circumstances. Understanding this can help you set realistic expectations for yourself and foster a forgiving mindset towards your parenting journey.

In the landscape of solo parenting, emotional outbursts or disagreements with your child can feel particularly intense. Without another adult to lean on or tag in when patience wears thin, these moments can escalate, affecting your and your child's emotional well-being. To manage this, proactive communication is vital. This involves regular conversations with your child about emotions and behaviors, using age-appropriate language to discuss why rules are in place and how certain behaviors affect both of you. These conversations can help your child understand the family dynamics more clearly, fostering a cooperative rather than confrontational atmosphere.

Building a Support Network

While the immediate family unit might be smaller for solo parents, this doesn't mean you have to manage alone. Building a support network is crucial and can significantly ease the pressures of solo parenting. This network could include family members, friends, fellow parents, or community members who can offer emotional support and practical help. For instance, arranging playdates with other parents can provide your child with social interaction and give you a much-needed breather or the opportunity to run errands.

Local parenting or support groups can also be invaluable, often found through social media platforms or community centers. These groups offer a space to share experiences, advice, and sometimes even childcare responsibilities. For example, a childcare co-op where parents take turns looking after each other's children can be a practical solution that builds community and mutual support.

Self-Care for Solo Parents

Self-care is often touted as a panacea for all stress, but for solo parents, it's not just beneficial; it's essential. Maintaining your emotional regulation is crucial for your well-being and as a model for your child. Self-care can be as simple as ensuring you get enough sleep, eat well, and find small pockets of time for activities that rejuvenate you. It might mean waking up 30 minutes before your child to enjoy a quiet cup of coffee or practicing a nighttime meditation to ensure restful sleep. Remember, self-care isn't selfish; it's necessary to keep you emotionally available and resilient for your child.

Additionally, consider professional help if you feel overwhelmed. A therapist can offer strategies to manage stress and cope with the emotional demands of solo parenting. This professional support can provide you with tools to stay emotionally grounded, helping you navigate your and your child's emotional landscapes more effectively.

Strategies for Effective Solo Parent Co-Regulation

Effective co-regulation as a solo parent involves creating a consistent routine that provides a predictable and secure environment for your child. Routines help manage expectations and reduce stress for both you and your child. These routines incorporate rituals that foster connection, such as reading a book together every night or having a special weekend breakfast. These moments of connection are crucial for reinforcing your emotional bond and providing your child with stability and reassurance.

Regarding discipline, focus on strategies that promote understanding and growth rather than punitive measures. Techniques such as time-ins, where you spend time together discussing emotions and behaviors, can be more effective than time-outs, which might make your child feel isolated. Always explain the reasons behind rules and the consequences of actions, and involve your child in setting family rules. This involvement can increase their commitment to these rules and reduce behavioral issues.

Balancing discipline with connection might seem like walking a tightrope, but you can navigate this path with clear communication, consistent routines, and a focus on emotional support. Remember, the goal of co-regulation is not just to manage behavior but to build a strong, emotionally intelligent foundation for your child, one where they feel secure, valued, and connected, even within the unique dynamics of solo parenting.

8.3 Navigating Major Life Changes: Moving, Divorce, and Loss

In its unpredictable flow, life brings significant changes that can turn a family's world upside down. Whether it's the emotional upheaval of a divorce, the physical dislocation of a move, or the deep grief accompanying the loss of a loved one, these events challenge the fabric of family life. During such times, children look to their parents for cues to react and cope. Your role in helping them navigate these waters is crucial, and it begins with understanding the profound impact these changes can have on their emotional world.

Supporting children through these transitions involves more than just a reassuring hug; it requires a strategic and compassionate approach that addresses their emotional and psychological needs. Start by acknowledging their feelings about the change. Children may not always verbalize their emotions directly, but signs of stress, anxiety, or sadness can manifest in changes in behavior, sleep patterns, or even appetite. Create opportunities for open dialogue, encouraging them to express their thoughts and emotions about the change. This could be facilitated through activities such as drawing, storytelling, or other forms of play, which often help younger children communicate what they might not yet have the words to say. For older children, direct conversations, perhaps during a walk or over a meal, can provide them with a safe space to express their feelings.

When discussing these life changes, be honest but also age-appropriate in your explanations. For instance, in the case of a divorce, you might explain that while the family's living arrangements might change, the love both parents have for the child remains constant. Reinforce this with consistent reassurance, affirming your unwavering support and love, which can help mitigate feelings of instability or insecurity they might be experiencing. Your steady presence and open communication are pillars they can lean on.

Maintaining Routines Amidst Change

The power of routine in providing stability during turbulent times cannot be overstated. Routines offer predictability in a world that, from a child's perspective, might suddenly seem bewilderingly chaotic. Strive to maintain regular schedules for meals, bedtime, and other daily activities as much as possible. If you're moving to a new home, quickly establish a new routine that mirrors the old one to help ease the transition. Keep familiar rituals, even small ones like reading a bedtime story or having a weekend breakfast, which can be comforting reminders that not everything has changed.

Maintaining daily routines can be challenging but essential in cases of loss, such as the death of a family member. It might be tempting to let typical structures slide during grief, but routines can act as anchors, helping children feel more secure. They also ensure that your child has a structured framework around which they can organize their experiences and expectations, providing a sense of continuity that is comforting in the face of loss.

Open Communication and Reassurance

Open communication fosters an environment where children feel safe to express their fears and uncertainties. Regularly check in with them to see how they adjust to the change. This doesn't need to be a formal sit-down conversation; casual yet attentive chats can encourage them to share their thoughts and feelings. Validate their emotions by listening attentively and acknowledging their right to feel upset, confused, or angry about the changes. Avoid platitudes that might diminish their feelings, such as "everything will be fine," without addressing their specific concerns.

Reassurance goes hand in hand with communication. Children need to know that they are not alone in navigating these changes. Reaffirm your presence and support, ensuring they understand they can rely on you for stability and guidance. This might involve more frequent expressions of love and support, extra patience as they adjust, and a proactive approach to spending quality time together.

Seeking Professional Support When Needed

Sometimes, the emotional complexity of significant life changes can overwhelm children and the entire family. Recognizing when you need outside help shows strength and proactive care. Therapists and counselors specializing in child psychology can give your child the tools to process their emotions healthily and constructively. They offer a neutral space for your child to express feelings they might hesitate to disclose to a parent, either from a desire not to cause further distress or from fear of repercussion.

School counselors can also be a valuable resource, mainly because they observe your child in a different environment and might notice changes in behavior or mood that aren't as apparent at home. Furthermore, consider support groups for children going through similar changes, such as groups for kids experiencing parental divorce or the death of a close family member. These groups can help normalize their emotions and provide peer support, which can be incredibly comforting.

Navigating your family through the turbulent waters of significant life changes is a profound challenge, requiring a blend of empathy, strategic planning, and sometimes professional guidance. By maintaining open lines of communication, reinforcing routines, and ensuring emotional support, you provide your child with the tools and stability needed to adjust to new realities, fostering resilience and emotional growth. This proactive and loving approach is vital in helping them emerge from these transitions stronger and more secure in their place in the family and the world.

8.4 Addressing Special Emotional Needs: ADHD, Autism, and Sensory Processing Issues

Children with ADHD, autism, and sensory processing issues bring a vibrant spectrum of challenges and strengths to our families. Understanding these special emotional needs is crucial in fostering a supportive environment that promotes their growth and well-being. Children with ADHD often experience difficulties with sustained attention, impulsivity, and hyperactivity, which can affect their emotional regulation and social interactions. Those with autism may face challenges in communication, social skills, and repetitive behaviors, alongside unique sensory sensitivities that influence how they perceive and interact with the world. Similarly, children with sensory processing issues might display extreme reactions to sensory stimuli, significantly impacting their emotional responses and behavior.

Tailoring co-regulation strategies to meet these needs involves a thoughtful blend of structure, consistency, and clear communication. For children with ADHD, structured routines coupled with clear, concise instructions can help manage their day-to-day activities and reduce feelings of overwhelm or frustration. Visual aids such as charts or color-coded schedules can provide tangible reminders of what is expected, helping to direct their focus and energy positively. Additionally, incorporating regular physical activity can significantly benefit children with ADHD, providing an outlet for excess energy and improving concentration.

For children on the autism spectrum, predictability and routine are comforting and essential. Unexpected changes can be distressing; hence, maintaining a consistent schedule and introducing new activities gradually can help mitigate anxiety. Communication strategies should be adapted to fit their level of understanding. They include using visual supports like picture cards or social stories that help explain social nuances and expected behaviors in various settings. Moreover, creating a sensory-friendly environment by being mindful of sensory triggers such as loud noises or bright lights can significantly affect how comfortable and calm these children feel.

Incorporating recommendations from healthcare professionals is vital in optimizing co-regulation practices for children with special needs. Collaborating with pediatricians, therapists, and exceptional education professionals can provide valuable insights into the most effective strategies tailored to each child's unique profile. These specialists can offer guidance on therapeutic approaches, educational interventions, and support resources that enhance the child's and the family's ability to manage and thrive despite the challenges. Regular consultations and follow-ups with these professionals ensure that the strategies remain effective and are adapted as the child grows and their needs evolve.

Building a supportive learning and living environment promotes emotional growth and stability. For children with sensory processing issues, this might include creating quiet corners where they can retreat when overwhelmed or integrating sensory play activities that help them regulate their sensory intake. Activities involving different textures, sounds, and visual stimuli can be therapeutic and fun, providing safe ways for these children to explore their sensory preferences and aversions. For all children with special needs, ensuring their environment is physically and emotionally safe is paramount. This includes fostering a home atmosphere of acceptance and understanding, where differences are celebrated, and challenges are met with empathy and support.

In conclusion, embracing the unique needs of children with ADHD, autism, and sensory processing issues with informed, compassionate co-regulation strategies enriches their development and familial bonds. It's a dynamic process that adjusts over time, always with the child's best interests at heart, ensuring they feel understood, supported, and loved.

8.5 Rebuilding After Breakdowns: Repairing the Connection

Every parent knows that emotional breakdowns happen even in the warmest of families. They could stem from a miscommunication, a disciplinary measure, or even the end of a particularly stressful day. Understandably, these moments can lead to rifts between you and your child, but they also provide powerful opportunities for growth and deeper connection. The key lies in effective repair strategies, which help mend the emotional gaps and restore trust and understanding in your relationship.

The process of repairing a relationship begins by acknowledging the emotions involved. Recognizing and validating your child's feelings and your own is essential. This might mean sitting down together and openly discussing what happened without judgment or defensiveness. You might say, "I noticed you were upset earlier; I was upset, too." Such acknowledgment doesn't just show empathy; it teaches your child how to recognize and express emotions constructively. Following this, a sincere apology can be incredibly powerful. Apologizing shows your child that everyone, even parents, can make mistakes and that taking responsibility for one's actions is a sign of strength, not weakness. It also teaches them about the value of humility and forgiveness.

Once feelings are acknowledged and apologies are made, discuss how similar situations might be handled better with your child. This could involve brainstorming solutions together, which helps prevent future breakdowns and empowers your child by involving them in the decision-making process. For instance, if a breakdown occurred over homework frustrations, you might agree on a signal your child can give when they feel overwhelmed, prompting a break or a change in activity. By turning challenges into collaborative problem-solving opportunities, you reinforce that difficulties are not roadblocks but catalysts for growth and learning.

Maintaining an open line of communication is crucial, not just in the aftermath of a breakdown but as a consistent practice. Encourage your child to express their feelings and concerns regularly. Set aside time each day for open-ended conversations, where questions like "How are you feeling about what happened at school today?" or "Is there anything on your mind you'd like to talk about?" become the norm. This ongoing dialogue keeps the emotional channels open, reducing the likelihood of misunderstandings and fostering an atmosphere where you can feel safe and supported in sharing your thoughts and feelings.

Embracing these strategies after emotional breakdowns transforms these challenging moments into valuable learning experiences and opportunities for emotional growth. It enhances the resilience of your parent-child relationship, ensuring that both of you know how to navigate conflicts healthily and effectively. By consistently applying these approaches, you foster a family dynamic rooted in mutual respect, understanding, and unconditional love, setting the stage for a lifelong bond built on a solid emotional foundation.

This chapter's exploration of strategies for repairing connections not only strengthens individual relationships but also contributes to the overall emotional health of the family. As we move forward, empathy, communication, and collaborative problem-solving principles will continue to play a crucial role in fostering an environment where every family member feels valued, understood, and supported.

Chapter 9:
Extending Beyond the Family

Imagine stepping into your child's classroom, a space buzzing with youthful energy and the promise of learning. Picture this environment as a seamless extension of your home's nurturing atmosphere, where emotional intelligence is as valued as academic success. This vision is a hopeful ideal and a practical possibility when co-regulation strategies bridge the gap between home and school settings. As a parent, your involvement doesn't end at the school gate; instead, it evolves into a collaborative partnership with educators, ensuring that your child receives consistent emotional support that significantly enhances their stability and capacity for learning.

9.1 Co-Regulation in the Classroom: Strategies for Teachers and Parents

Bridging Home and School Environments

The continuity of emotional support from home to school is critical for your child's emotional stability and overall development. Consistent co-regulation strategies between these two vital environments help your child navigate the school's academic and social challenges with greater ease and confidence. This consistency ensures that the child perceives both home and school as safe and supportive spaces to express themselves and manage their emotions healthily. For this seamless transition, it is crucial for you, as a parent, to communicate openly with your child's educators about the emotional strategies you use at home. Sharing insights about what calms your child, what triggers their stress, or how they best receive positive reinforcement enables teachers to provide more tailored emotional support that aligns with your child's needs.

Teacher-Parent Collaboration

Effective collaboration between you and your child's teachers can significantly enhance the emotional and educational support your child receives. This partnership is built on regular, open communication and mutual respect for roles in your child's life. Initiating this collaborative relationship can begin with setting up a meeting at the start of the school year to discuss your child's emotional and learning needs. Regular follow-ups through emails, calls, or parent-teacher conferences can continue to foster this relationship. Additionally, participating in school activities and volunteering in the classroom can give you insights into the school environment and build stronger relationships with the educational staff. This involvement shows your child that you value their educational experience and are actively supporting their academic and emotional growth.

Training for Educators

While many educators are skilled in instructional strategies, specific training in co-regulation can further enhance their ability to manage classroom dynamics and effectively support children's emotional learning. Advocating for and supporting co-regulation training programs within schools can equip teachers with the tools to help students manage their emotions, reduce classroom conflicts, and create a more supportive learning environment. These programs can teach educators techniques such as recognizing emotional triggers in students, using calming techniques, and integrating emotional health into the curriculum. When teachers are trained to co-regulate effectively, they contribute to a more positive classroom climate and model emotional intelligence skills that students, including your child, can learn from and emulate.

Creating Emotionally Supportive Classrooms

The structure and routine of the classroom play a pivotal role in fostering co-regulation among students. Teachers can create an emotionally supportive atmosphere by establishing clear, predictable routines that make students feel secure and engaged. For instance, starting each day with a brief mindfulness exercise can help students center their emotions and prepare for learning. Visual schedules and clearly defined classroom rules can reduce anxiety by clarifying expectations. Furthermore, creating a 'cool-down' corner equipped with calming tools like stress balls, books, or soft music can provide a safe space for students to manage their emotions and regain control before rejoining classroom activities. These strategies support individual emotional regulation and enhance overall classroom management, making the classroom a more inclusive and empathetic space for all students.

Integrating these strategies into the classroom benefits your child and fosters a broader culture of emotional intelligence and respect among all students. By bridging the gap between home and school environments, facilitating solid partnerships with educators, supporting targeted training, and advocating for emotionally supportive classroom practices, you play a crucial role in shaping an educational experience that values and nurtures emotional well-being as much as academic achievement. This holistic approach ensures that the classroom extends the supportive, emotionally intelligent environment you strive to provide at home, creating a consistent and stable foundation for your child's growth and learning.

9.2 Building a Supportive Parenting Community: Finding and Creating Your Tribe

Navigating the complexities of parenting, especially when aiming to foster environments of emotional intelligence and co-regulation, can sometimes feel like an isolating journey. However, the power of community support in this aspect cannot be overstated. A supportive parenting community offers a network of insights, shared experiences, and mutual encouragement, which can significantly lighten the emotional load of parenting. These communities provide a platform for exchanging strategies that have worked for others, potentially offering solutions you might have yet to consider. Additionally, such networks foster a sense of belonging and understanding, which is crucial for parents who might otherwise feel alone in their challenges.

Finding your parenting tribe, a group of like-minded individuals who share your values and parenting goals, can be a transformative experience. Start by looking for local parenting groups in your community. These might be found through social media platforms, local community centers, or schools. Attending local events, workshops, and talks on parenting can also connect you with individuals with a similar focus on co-regulation and emotional intelligence. Online communities can be equally beneficial for those needing access to active local groups. Numerous forums, social media groups, and parenting websites offer spaces to discuss and learn from others' experiences. When searching for these groups, look for keywords that align with your parenting values, such as "emotional intelligence in parenting," "co-regulation with children," or "mindful parenting." Engaging in these groups by asking questions, sharing experiences, and offering insights can help solidify your presence and establish meaningful connections.

Creating your own support group can be rewarding if existing groups do not meet your expectations or if you're looking for something more specific to your needs. Begin by identifying what you aim to achieve through this group. Whether it's focusing on specific age groups, tackling unique challenges such as parenting in single-parent households, or emphasizing co-regulation techniques, having a clear focus will attract parents with similar interests. You can use local community bulletin boards, social media platforms, or school newsletters to invite interested parents. Organize an initial meeting in a casual, welcoming environment to discuss the group's goals, structure, and potential activities. Regular meetings can be scheduled based on what works best for the group members, and activities include guest speakers, book discussions, and sharing sessions where members can talk about their successes and challenges in a supportive setting.

The importance of open sharing and learning from one another within these communities cannot be understated. Encourage an atmosphere where members feel safe to express their vulnerabilities without fear of judgment. This openness helps build trust and enriches the learning experience, as parents feel more comfortable sharing their unique insights and strategies. Facilitate discussions that allow members to explore different perspectives and learn new approaches to parenting challenges. This might involve structured sharing sessions, where each member focuses on a particular topic of interest, allowing members to prepare thoughts and experiences to share. Inviting experts to speak on subjects of interest, such as child psychologists or experienced educators, can provide professional insights and add substantial value to the group's interactions.

By fostering a supportive community, you enhance your parenting journey and contribute to a more significant movement of emotional intelligence and thoughtful parenting. These networks create a ripple effect, as every parent who benefits from this support is likely to foster better emotional health and co-regulation within their own family, thereby gradually influencing broader community interactions with these foundational skills. In this way, a simple gathering of like-minded parents can grow into a powerful force for positive change, enhancing the well-being of families and communities alike.

9.3 Advocating for Your Child: Effective Communication with Educators and Professionals

Navigating the educational and healthcare systems can sometimes feel like moving through a maze with various turns and dead ends, particularly when advocating for your child's needs. Understanding your child's rights within these systems is not just beneficial; instead, it's also empowering. In educational settings, children have the right to access learning opportunities that cater to their individual needs, whether these are special accommodations for disabilities or support for gifted education programs. Familiarizing yourself with these rights, often outlined in educational policies and federal laws like the Individuals with Disabilities Education Act (IDEA) in the United States, equips you with the knowledge to ensure these rights are respected and implemented. This understanding forms the bedrock of effective advocacy, providing a clear framework within which you can operate to support your child's educational journey.

The approach is as important as the message when advocating for your child. Start by establishing a clear and open line of communication with teachers, administrators, and healthcare providers from the outset. Schedule regular meetings or communications to discuss your child's progress, challenges, and any observations from home that might be pertinent. It's crucial to approach these interactions as a partnership rather than a confrontation. Express appreciation for the professional's efforts and frame your concerns as shared goals for the best outcomes for your child. For instance, if your child needs more challenge in a particular subject, discuss this by highlighting your child's enthusiasm and rapid learning pace, suggesting that adjustments might benefit their engagement and growth.

Documentation is your ally. Keep detailed records of all communications, including emails, meeting notes, and reports. This documentation can be invaluable when you must follow up on specific agreements or advocate for additional services. If your child has an Individualized Education Program (IEP), maintaining a copy of this document and all evaluations, reports, and correspondence related to it helps ensure that all parties are on the same page and that your child's needs are being met consistently with their rights.

Navigating potentially challenging conversations is an art that often requires as much emotional intelligence as factual preparation. When disagreements arise, or you must assert your child's rights more firmly, remain calm and focused. Use factual statements and refer to documentation to support your points. For example, if a promised support service has not been initiated, calmly reference the agreed start date from previous communications, expressing concern for your child's need for this service. If these conversations do not yield the desired results, do not hesitate to escalate your concerns appropriately, including seeking mediation or legal advice, particularly when it involves ensuring compliance with legal rights.

Building productive, cooperative relationships with educators and healthcare professionals is pivotal. These relationships are built on mutual respect, regular communication, and a shared commitment to your child's well-being and development. Participate in school and community events to strengthen these relationships and show your support for the educational environment. Offering your skills and time in areas that align with your profession or hobbies can provide additional opportunities to engage with and support the educational team.

Advocating effectively for your child involves a balanced approach of collaboration, clear communication, and, when necessary, firm negotiation. By understanding your child's rights, maintaining open lines of communication with professionals, and approaching advocacy as a partnership, you empower your child and yourself as a parent, ensuring that your child's educational and developmental needs are met with the attention and respect they deserve. This proactive and informed approach lays a strong foundation for your child's success and well-being in any educational or professional setting, reinforcing the importance of advocacy in navigating the complexities of modern education and healthcare systems.

9.4 Digital Citizenship: Teaching Kids to Navigate Online Interactions with Empathy

In today's landscape, where the digital realm often mirrors and sometimes even surpasses interactions in the physical world, digital citizenship becomes crucial. Digital citizenship refers to the responsible use of technology by anyone who engages online, encompassing aspects of online etiquette, privacy, sharing, and community involvement. For children, becoming adept digital citizens means learning to navigate the complexities of online interactions with the same integrity and respect expected in face-to-face encounters.

This understanding is essential, not only for their safety but also for their emotional and social development.

Teaching children to navigate online interactions with empathy, respect, and understanding is multifaceted. It begins with modeling. As in all areas of child development, children learn a great deal from observing the behaviors of adults. Regular discussions about your online interactions and the decisions you make about what to share and how to respond to others online can provide practical examples that children can learn from. Furthermore, it's beneficial to involve children in setting up their social media profiles or email accounts, discussing each step, from choosing what personal information to share to selecting privacy settings. This hands-on approach makes the concepts of digital citizenship more tangible. It allows you to address potential scenarios they might encounter, discussing how empathy and respect can guide their responses.

Another effective strategy is to use real-life scenarios to teach these principles. You can create hypothetical situations or use anonymized examples from news stories to discuss with your child. Questions like "What would you do if you saw someone being bullied online?" or "How would you react if someone shared a rumor about a classmate?" help prompt discussion. These conversations help children understand the impact of their actions and the importance of thinking critically about the content they encounter or share online. Role-playing can also be a dynamic way to practice these skills, allowing children to think through their actions and consider the feelings of others, thereby reinforcing the importance of empathy in digital interactions.

Managing online conflicts effectively is another critical component of digital citizenship. Conflicts might arise from misunderstandings or even the perceived tone in text-based communication, which needs more non-verbal cues of face-to-face interactions. Teaching children to step back and assess the situation before responding can prevent many conflicts from escalating. Encourage them to contact a trusted adult if they're unsure how to handle a problem or if the conflict intensifies. This guidance can help them feel supported rather than overwhelmed by online disputes. Additionally, discussing the importance of not engaging in or encouraging cyberbullying and understanding the permanence and public nature of online interactions is essential. These discussions can help children understand the long-term consequences of their actions online.

Setting healthy boundaries around digital use is equally important to ensure that children's online interactions remain positive and do not interfere with real-world relationships or responsibilities. This involves creating rules about when and where devices can be used, how long children can spend online, and what types of activities are appropriate. For instance, no devices during family meals or turning off screens at least an hour before bedtime can be part of your family's digital etiquette. Encouraging activities without screens is also helpful, as it provides children with a healthy balance and helps them value face-to-face interactions. Periodic reviews of their browsing history and discussions about the content they access can also maintain an open line of communication about their online activities. By setting these boundaries and monitoring their adherence, you help your child develop self-discipline and make informed choices about their digital engagement, fostering a balanced approach to online and offline life.

In teaching digital citizenship, the goal is to equip children with the skills to engage online thoughtfully, empathetically, and safely, ensuring their digital interactions are as enriching and respectful as those in person.

9.5 The Ripple Effect: How Co-Regulation Can Transform Communities

Imagine a community where principles of empathy, understanding, and mutual support guide every interaction, every meeting, and every communal effort. This is the essence of incorporating co-regulation into community values, a practice that transcends the boundaries of individual families and influences the broader social fabric. When communities embrace co-regulation, they cultivate environments where every member, regardless of age, feels understood, valued, and connected. This shift can lead to transformative changes in social dynamics, reducing conflicts and fostering a collective sense of well-being and cooperation.

The potential impact of adopting co-regulation as a widely practiced community value is profound. Co-regulation involves managing one's emotions and behaviors in ways that positively affect others, promoting a more empathetic community interaction. For instance, community meetings that incorporate principles of co-regulation can become more productive and inclusive. In such meetings, members would be encouraged to express their thoughts and emotions openly, with the assurance that their inputs are valued. This practice enhances individual participation and builds a collective decision-making process that reflects the community's diverse needs and aspirations.

Furthermore, when communities commit to practicing co-regulation, they set the stage for future generations to inherit and further these values. Children and young people observing adults engage in empathetic and regulated interactions learn to replicate these behaviors. Schools, local clubs, and youth groups can reinforce these lessons, incorporating co-regulation into their programs and activities. Over time, this generational learning can significantly alter community norms, embedding empathy and emotional intelligence in the community's culture.

Highlighting examples of community initiatives that have successfully implemented co-regulation principles can provide both inspiration and a blueprint for action. Consider a community center that introduces a program where older residents mentor young people, sharing life skills and providing emotional support. These intergenerational interactions can enhance understanding and respect between age groups, each learning from the other's experiences and perspectives. Another example could be local health services organizing workshops on emotional regulation and mental health, open to all community members. These workshops could cover stress management, effective communication, and conflict resolution, equipping residents with skills to improve their personal and communal lives.

Encouraging empathy and understanding through community activities or programs strengthens communal bonds. Organizing regular community events that bring diverse groups together is one way to foster a more inclusive atmosphere. Events could range from cultural festivals celebrating different community heritages to town hall meetings focusing on community issues and solutions. During these events, structured activities requiring cooperative efforts, like community gardening or neighborhood clean-ups, can further promote mutual understanding and shared responsibility.

Building a more compassionate society is the natural progression of widespread co-regulation practice. This societal change doesn't occur overnight but evolves through consistent and collective effort across various community interactions. By valuing and practicing co-regulation, communities enhance the immediate social environment and contribute to a broader cultural shift towards greater empathy and compassion. This shift can lead to more supportive social policies, improved mental health, and a stronger sense of community, where people feel they are part of something larger than themselves, committed to mutual well-being and support.

As this chapter draws to a close, we reflect on the transformative power of co-regulation within families and entire communities. By adopting co-regulation as a critical community value, fostering initiatives that support this practice, and encouraging empathy and understanding in communal interactions, we pave the way for a society that values emotional intelligence and mutual respect. These efforts promise a ripple effect, where today's practice of co-regulation leads to tomorrow's norm of compassionate and empathetic community living. As we move forward, let us carry these insights into the next chapter, exploring the future of co-regulation and its potential to shape a more emotionally intelligent, understanding, and connected world.

Chapter 10:
The Future of Co-Regulation

Imagine a quiet evening where, instead of the usual rush to manage dinner and homework amidst the echoes of the day's stress, you deeply engage in a calm, constructive conversation with your pre-teen about their school day. This scenario, rich with emotional connection and mutual understanding, isn't a distant dream but a realistic outcome of evolving your co-regulation strategies as your child grows. This chapter delves into the dynamic nature of parent-child relationships and the essential adaptations in co-regulation that you can apply to foster an emotionally resilient family ready to face the changing tides of growth and development.

10.1 The Evolving Parent-Child Relationship: Adapting Co-Regulation Strategies as Children Grow

Dynamic nature of co-regulation

Co-regulation is not a static skill but an evolving interaction that shifts as your child grows from the tender stages of toddlerhood through the exploratory teenage years and beyond. Initially, co-regulation might guide your toddler through a tantrum with gentle words and a calming embrace. However, their emotional and cognitive landscapes expand dramatically as children enter school age. They encounter complex social situations and academic challenges requiring a refined co-regulation approach. Here, your role shifts subtly from direct management to more of a guiding presence, offering strategies and insights while encouraging them to apply these tools independently.

Navigating developmental stages

Each developmental stage brings unique challenges and opportunities for emotional growth. For instance, school-aged children develop a sharper sense of self-awareness and a burgeoning understanding of others' perspectives. This stage is a critical period for reinforcing the skills of empathy and self-regulation. Activities like role-playing can be effective, allowing children to practice responding to various emotional scenarios in a safe, controlled environment. As they step into the complexities of adolescence, the strategies for co-regulation require further adaptation. Teenagers striving for independence might resist overt guidance. Here, co-regulation involves more dialogue, asking insightful questions, and listening actively, allowing the teen to conclude about managing emotions and relationships.

Maintaining connection through changes

Despite these changes, the core of effective co-regulation remains the emotional connection between you and your child. This connection is the lifeline through which trust, advice, and emotional wisdom are passed. Maintaining this connection doesn't always require grand gestures; regular, everyday interactions can serve as powerful conduits of emotional exchange. Simple practices such as sharing your day and inviting your child to discuss theirs can reinforce this bond. It's about creating an environment where emotions are acknowledged openly, discussed freely, and managed constructively.

Tools for adapting strategies

As your child matures, the tools and resources you employ to facilitate co-regulation must evolve. One effective tool is the emotional journal, which can be particularly beneficial as children grow into their teenage years. Encouraging your child to write about daily experiences and their feelings about these events can provide them with a private outlet for reflection and emotional processing. Maintaining an open dialogue about these entries can offer insights into your child's emotional world, helping you tailor your co-regulation strategies to their current needs. Additionally, technology can serve as a resource. There are apps designed to help manage anxiety and stress through mindfulness exercises, which can particularly appeal to tech-savvy teenagers. Introducing your child to these tools supports their independent emotional regulation and reinforces the ongoing nature of learning and adapting to emotional intelligence.

In this continuous growth journey, you and your child learn and adapt. The strategies evolve, but the goal remains to foster a relationship grounded in mutual understanding and emotional support. As you adjust your co-regulation approaches to meet your child's changing needs, you pave the way for them to enter adulthood with a robust set of emotional skills, ready to handle the complexities of their relationships and professional challenges. This evolving strategy is not just about preventing emotional upheavals but about enriching the familial bond, making every growth stage an opportunity to deepen connections and enhance mutual understanding.

10.2 Staying Connected in the Teen Years: Co-Regulation Through Adolescence

Adolescence is a period of profound change, where teenagers embark on the challenging journey towards independence, often marked by emotional upheavals and a quest for identity. This developmental stage brings unique challenges to co-regulation as teens increasingly assert their independence and sometimes resist parental guidance. Yet, during these years, maintaining a solid emotional connection becomes crucial, even as the dynamics of this connection transform. As you navigate this complex phase with your teen, understanding the subtleties of these changes can help you adapt your approach to co-regulation, ensuring that it remains effective and respectful of your teen's growing need for autonomy.

Co-regulation with teenagers involves a delicate balance between offering guidance and allowing independence, making open communication a critical component of this relationship. Fostering an environment where your teen feels safe to express their thoughts and feelings without fear of judgment or immediate repercussions is essential. This can be achieved by regular, informal conversations in a non-threatening space, perhaps during a car ride, while preparing a meal together, or on a walk. The key is to be present and genuinely interested in their point of view rather than ready with an immediate response or a solution to their issues. Active listening plays a vital role here; it involves more than just hearing their words; it's about understanding the emotions and intentions behind what is being said. This level of attentiveness shows your teen that their feelings and thoughts are valid and vital, fostering more profound mutual respect and understanding.

Supporting emotional autonomy in teens is about helping them develop their ability to regulate their own emotions and relationships. This support involves teaching them strategies to handle stress, conflict, and disappointment independently while reassuring them that guidance is available. One effective way to do this is through problem-solving discussions, where you guide your teen to think through various solutions to a problem, weigh their possible outcomes, and decide on the best course of action themselves. This process enhances their decision-making skills and boosts their confidence in their ability to handle challenges independently. Another strategy is encouraging them to engage in activities promoting emotional well-being, such as sports, arts, or volunteering. These activities provide outlets for expression and opportunities for self-discovery, which is essential for emotional maturity.

Respecting boundaries and privacy is crucial as teens grow more sensitive about their independence and personal space. This respect is a foundational aspect of trust and plays a significant role in how teens perceive their relationship with their parents. Negotiating boundaries that protect their privacy while ensuring they are safe and responsible is essential. This might mean having agreed-upon times when you don't intrude on their space without permission or setting parameters around technology use that respect their privacy while safeguarding them from potential online risks. Discussions about these boundaries should be collaborative, inviting your teen to participate in creating rules that affect their life. This makes them feel respected and teaches them about the responsibilities that come with greater autonomy.

In essence, navigating the teen years requires shifting from more directive forms of co-regulation to a more collaborative and advisory role. This shift is crucial for maintaining your connection during these challenging years and equipping your teen with the emotional tools they need to thrive as independent adults. By focusing on open communication, supporting emotional autonomy, and respecting growing boundaries, you build a strong foundation of trust and understanding to guide your relationship with your teenager through adolescence and beyond. As you adjust your strategies to meet the evolving needs of your teen, remember that every step forward, no matter how small, is a part of their more extraordinary journey towards emotional maturity and independence.

10.3 The Long-Term Impact of Co-Regulation: Insights from Research and Real Life Scenarios

Research findings on co-regulation

Novel research has begun illuminating the profound impacts of well-implemented co-regulation practices on children, stretching far into their adult lives. Studies conducted across various demographics have consistently shown that children who experience effective co-regulation are more likely to develop robust emotional regulation skills. This skill set is crucial for personal well-being and for forming stable, healthy relationships in adulthood. One significant longitudinal study tracked children from early childhood through to their thirties and found that those who had been taught to manage emotions effectively were better at handling interpersonal conflicts, had lower levels of psychological stress, and reported higher overall life satisfaction. These findings underscore the critical role that nurturing emotional intelligence from an early age plays in shaping an individual's ability to navigate the complexities of adult relationships and professional environments. Furthermore, these individuals often exhibit enhanced problem-solving skills, a trait linked to emotional agility and resilience. This research provides compelling evidence supporting co-regulation integration into early parenting and educational practices, positioning it not merely as beneficial but essential for fostering long-term emotional health and societal well-being.

Personal stories of impact

Beyond the numbers and data, the real-life stories of individuals who have benefited from co-regulation practices bring a human face to the statistics. Consider the story of Elena, a young woman who credits her ability to navigate a particularly challenging professional environment to the co-regulation skills her parents instilled in her. From an early age, her parents engaged her in discussions about her feelings, teaching her to name her emotions and work through them constructively. This early education in emotional intelligence became a cornerstone of her personal and professional success, allowing her to maintain composure and empathy in high-stress situations. These traits eventually earned her a leadership position at her firm. Another example is Marco, who grew up in a household where co-regulation was a daily practice. His ability to understand and manage his emotions helped him through personal losses and challenges, illustrating how these skills are not just about improving immediate family dynamics but are crucial tools for lifelong resilience and emotional health.

Benefits beyond the family

The ripple effects of co-regulation extend beyond individual and familial benefits, touching broader societal and community levels.

Communities where co-regulation practices are widespread experience lower levels of conflict and higher degrees of social cohesion. Schools where teachers and staff are trained in emotional co-regulation techniques typically have fewer disciplinary incidents and a more inclusive atmosphere. These environments encourage students from various backgrounds to engage more fully, promoting a culture of empathy and mutual respect. Furthermore, workplaces that embrace emotional intelligence often report better teamwork, lower employee turnover, and higher job satisfaction. These broader societal benefits highlight the potential of co-regulation practices to foster communities where understanding and cooperation are the norms, contributing to a more harmonious social fabric.

Future directions for co-regulation research

Looking forward, the scope for research into co-regulation is vast and varied. Future studies could explore the specific impacts of co-regulation across different cultural contexts, examining how diverse parenting styles and societal norms influence the effectiveness of co-regulation techniques. Another promising area of research involves integrating technology in teaching and practicing co-regulation. With the rise of digital tools and platforms, there is potential to develop interactive applications that could assist parents and educators in implementing co-regulation strategies more effectively. Additionally, longitudinal studies that track the long-term outcomes of co-regulated individuals could provide deeper insights into how these practices affect health, career success, and interpersonal relationships over decades. By continuing to explore these areas, researchers can refine co-regulation practices and better understand their potential to contribute to a healthier, more empathetic society.

10.4 Co-Regulation and Society: Envisioning a More Empathetic World

The fabric of society is intricately woven from the threads of individual interactions, each colored by the emotional and communicative skills of its participants. Imagine a society where co-regulation is not just a practice confined to family dynamics but a fundamental aspect of all social interactions. The widespread adoption of co-regulation across various societal contexts promises to foster a more empathetic and understanding world. This vision is not merely aspirational but grounded in the potential for real and substantial societal transformation. By extending co-regulation practices beyond the home into schools, workplaces, and community institutions, the very framework of social interaction can be reshaped to promote greater empathy, reduce conflicts, and enhance collaborative efforts.

In educational settings, the infusion of co-regulation practices can revolutionize the traditional dynamics between students and educators. Schools serve as the initial social crucible where young individuals learn to navigate complex social waters. Embedding co-regulation into the curriculum can provide students with early exposure to emotional intelligence skills, equipping them with the tools needed to manage their emotions and understand those of others. This approach not only aids in personal development but also creates a more supportive and inclusive school environment. Teachers trained in co-regulation can implement strategies that help students cope with stress, resolve conflicts amicably, and support their peers, laying the groundwork for a more compassionate generation.

Transitioning to the workplace, co-regulation principles can significantly enhance organizational culture and efficiency. In a professional environment, where stress levels can be high and interpersonal conflicts frequent, co-regulation is a critical skill set promoting a cooperative atmosphere. Companies prioritizing emotional intelligence training and co-regulation practices report higher employee satisfaction, improved teamwork, and increased productivity. These workplaces become models of emotional health, demonstrating how understanding and managing emotions can lead to more effective communication and better problem-solving. Encouraging businesses to adopt these practices through incentives and training programs can propagate the benefits of co-regulation across the economic spectrum, contributing to a more harmonious and productive society.

On a broader scale, co-regulation principles can influence public policy, particularly in areas such as education, healthcare, and urban development. Policymakers can integrate co-regulation into educational policies by mandating emotional intelligence programs in schools, thus fostering an emotionally aware citizenry. In healthcare, policies that encourage training medical professionals in emotional intelligence can enhance patient care and improve the mental health of the community. Urban development can also benefit from co-regulation by designing public spaces promoting social interaction and community activities, strengthening communal bonds. These policy initiatives can catalyze widespread societal change, embedding co-regulation into communities' structural and cultural fabric.

For you, as a parent, the practice and promotion of co-regulation offer a unique opportunity to leave a lasting legacy of empathy. By embodying and teaching these principles, you contribute to the emotional well-being of your family and the broader community. Each interaction, whether a simple exchange in a local store or a discussion at a school meeting, becomes a chance to demonstrate and spread the values of empathy and mutual understanding. This ripple effect can gradually transform societal attitudes, paving the way for a future where co-regulation is recognized not as a specialized skill but as a fundamental aspect of human interaction. In this envisioned world, the legacy of empathy you cultivate within your family extends outward, influencing countless lives and shaping a society that values emotional connection and understanding above all.

10.5 Passing the Baton:
How to Teach Your Children About Emotional Intelligence and Co-Regulation

In the parenting landscape, teaching your children about emotional intelligence and co-regulation nuances is one of the most valuable gifts you can offer. This is not just about instructing them in managing their emotions but about equipping them with the skills to navigate life's complex social environments with empathy, resilience, and understanding. The task begins with you, their foremost role model. Your daily interactions, the emotional tone you set at home, and how you handle your own emotions provide the framework within which your children learn to engage with their feelings and those of others.

Educating children about emotional intelligence starts with demystifying emotions. It involves breaking down complex feelings into understandable parts, helping children recognize their feelings, and connecting them to their thoughts and actions. This can be as simple as having regular conversations about emotions and using moments of emotional distress or joy as opportunities for discussion. For example, after a disagreement with a friend, you might discuss with your child what they felt during the incident, what might have triggered those feelings, and how different reactions could change the outcome of similar situations. These discussions should highlight that all emotions are valid and that understanding and managing them is a skill they can develop over time. You can further enrich this learning by incorporating age-appropriate books and media that explore emotional themes, providing children with diverse perspectives on handling emotional situations.

As vital as providing knowledge about emotions, your role in modeling effective co-regulation and emotional intelligence is equally crucial. Children are astute observers, often mimicking the behaviors they see in their parents. This mimicry isn't limited to physical actions but extends to emotional responses. They are likelier to adopt these behaviors if they see you managing stress with calm and resilience or expressing joy and gratitude openly. Make a conscious effort to express your own emotions healthily and transparently. When you experience anger or frustration, verbalize these feelings and let your children see how you manage them. For instance, if you're frustrated by a work email, you might say, "I'm feeling quite frustrated by this message, so I'm going to take a few deep breaths to calm down before I respond." Such demonstrations can teach children practical ways to regulate emotions and communicate effectively.

Encouraging your children to be advocates for co-regulation and emotional intelligence among their peers involves instilling a sense of responsibility and leadership regarding emotional health. This can be fostered by encouraging them to share what they learn about emotions with friends or by involving them in peer mediation programs at school. These activities reinforce their learning and help them understand the impact of emotional intelligence on others. It's also beneficial to discuss scenarios they may encounter, such as a friend facing bullying or dealing with sadness, and brainstorm ways they might help their friend cope, perhaps by sharing techniques like deep breathing or seeking adult assistance.

Looking to the future, consider the legacy your practices around emotional intelligence and co-regulation will leave. This isn't just about your children managing their emotions effectively; it's about carrying forward values that prioritize empathy, understanding, and emotional connection. As they become adults and parents, the principles they've learned and observed in your home will influence how they interact with others, shape their relationships, and impact their communities. This long-term perspective underscores the importance of what you're teaching today; it's not merely a skill set for emotional management but a foundational philosophy for a kinder, more empathetic world.

In wrapping up this chapter, we've explored the multifaceted approach to teaching children about emotional intelligence and co-regulation. From engaging in open discussions about emotions and modeling effective emotional management to encouraging advocacy among peers and considering the long-term impact of these teachings, the strategies discussed here are designed to prepare your children not just for the challenges of today but for a lifetime of meaningful interpersonal interactions. As we move forward, the insights garnered here form the stepping stones to understanding how these practices can be further enhanced and tailored to meet children's and society's evolving needs.

Conclusion

As we reach the close of our journey through "Mastering Co-Regulation Parenting," I want to take a moment to reflect on the profound principles and transformative strategies we've explored together. This book has guided you in enhancing emotional intelligence within your family, synchronizing emotions between you and your child, and implementing practical strategies that foster a nurturing and empathetic family environment. The core principles of co-regulation parenting, centered around understanding and mutual empathy, are designed to strengthen your family dynamics and extend these benefits into broader societal contexts.

Throughout these pages, we've embarked on a continuous emotional growth and learning journey. Remember, mastering co-regulation is an evolving process that flourishes over time with dedication, practice, and patience. Both you and your children are on a path of mutual development, where each step forward enriches your understanding and connection.

The benefits of effective co-regulation extend far beyond the confines of your home. They ripple out into schools, communities, and the broader fabric of society, fostering environments rich in empathy and compassion. This is not just about improving family life; it's about contributing to a world where emotional intelligence and understanding prevail.

Please apply the strategies and insights from this book to your everyday interactions. Whether it's a challenging bedtime or a conflict resolution during a family meeting, your persistence in applying these principles can transform potential stress into moments of connection and growth. Adaptability and empathy are your allies in navigating the parenting landscape, helping you to meet each challenge with a heart and mindset poised for understanding and compassion.

As you continue to advocate for and practice co-regulation parenting, you become part of a more significant movement, a wave of change that enhances the emotional well-being of children and families everywhere. Share your experiences and insights with other parents and your community, inspiring them to join this transformative journey.

Now, as we conclude, I invite you to commit to this ongoing journey of co-regulation. Your efforts to nurture deep, empathetic relationships within your family are invaluable. They lay the foundation for your children's emotional development and the harmony of your family life. Reflect on the growth you've witnessed in yourself and your family since beginning this path. Celebrate the progress, no matter how small, and know each step contributes to a more robust, resilient family unit.

I understand that this path is not without its challenges, but every challenge overcome is a victory in building a robust, emotionally intelligent family. I am grateful for your dedication to enhancing your family's emotional journey, and I assure you this is just the beginning. For further guidance and support, I encourage you to engage with available resources, join parenting communities, and continue exploring literature that supports your growth in this vital aspect of parenting.

Thank you for allowing me to be a part of your journey. May the path you forge with co-regulation parenting lead to profound joy and deep, lasting connections within your family and beyond. Here's to a future where every family thrives in an atmosphere of understanding, empathy, and emotional intelligence.

References

- The Neuroscience of Emotion Regulation Development - NCBI
  https://www.ncbi.nlm.nih.gov/pmc/articles/PMC5096655/

- Attachment and child development
  https://learning.nspcc.org.uk/child-health
  development/attachment-early-years/

- Tips to Improve Family Relationships
  https://www.helpguide.org/articles/mental-health/improving-
  family-relationships-with-emotional-intelligence.htm

- Emotional Safety is Necessary for Emotional Connection
  https://www.gottman.com/blog/emotional-safety-is-necessary-
  for-emotional-connection/

- Effects of parental empathy and emotion regulation on
  https://www.ncbi.nlm.nih.gov/pmc/articles/PMC7331354/

- How to communicate effectively with your young child -
  UNICEF https://www.unicef.org/parenting/child-care/9-tips-
  for-better-communication

- Healthy Boundaries, Healthy Children
  https://www.edutopia.org/sites/default/files/resources/stw-
  glenview-healthy-boundaries.pdf

- The Effect of Parent Psychological Distress on Child
  https://www.ncbi.nlm.nih.gov/pmc/articles/PMC7758226/

- Enhancing Mental Health through Mindful Pause
  https://inbloomproject.com/blog-2/enhancing-mental-health-through-mindful-pause

- Simple Self-Care for Extremely Busy Parents
  https://imperfectfamilies.com/simple-self-care-for-extremely-busy-parents/

- Virtual Support Groups | Parents Helping Parents
  https://parentshelpingparents.org/virtual-support-groups

- Conceptualizing Emotion Regulation and Coregulation as
  https://www.ncbi.nlm.nih.gov/pmc/articles/PMC8801237/

- How to Handle Tantrums and Meltdowns
  https://childmind.org/article/how-to-handle-tantrums-and-meltdowns/

- Adolescent Mental Health in the Digital Age: Facts, Fears
  https://www.ncbi.nlm.nih.gov/pmc/articles/PMC8221420/

- Resilience guide for parents and teachers
  https://www.apa.org/topics/resilience/guide-parents-teachers

- The Importance of Play in Promoting Healthy Child Development
  https://publications.aap.org/pediatrics/article/119/1/182/70699/The-Importance-of-Play-in-Promoting-Healthy-Child

- Mindful Parenting: How to Respond Instead of React
  https://www.gottman.com/blog/mindful-parenting-how-to-respond-instead-of-react/

- Identifying the 5 Love Languages of Children
  https://www.thebump.com/a/love-languages-of-children
- Key Strategies to Teach Children Empathy (Sorted by Age)
  https://biglifejournal.com/blogs/blog/key-strategies-teach-children-empathy
- The generational impact of household clutter
  https://pubmed.ncbi.nlm.nih.gov/36478581/
- Routines and child development: A systematic review
  https://onlinelibrary.wiley.com/doi/full/10.1111/jftr.12549
- Improving Family Communications
  https://www.healthychildren.org/English/family-life/family-dynamics/communication-discipline/Pages/Improving-Family-Communications.aspx
- A literature review of gratitude, parent–child relationships
  https://www.sciencedirect.com/science/article/abs/pii/S0273229721000034
- Routines and child development: A systematic review
  https://onlinelibrary.wiley.com/doi/full/10.1111/jftr.12549
- 10 Tips to Reduce Homework Stress
  https://www.oxfordlearning.com/how-to-reduce-homework-stress/
- Effects of Excessive Screen Time on Child Development - NCBI
  https://www.ncbi.nlm.nih.gov/pmc/articles/PMC10353947/

- Eating Together as a Family: 10 Emotional Health Benefits
  https://thenourishedchild.com/benefits-eating-together-as-a-family/
- Five Strategies to Improve Parent-Child Communication
  https://www.ourfamilywizard.com/blog/five-strategies-improve-parent-child-communication
- 7 Single-Parent Support Systems
  https://www.care.com/c/7-single-parent-support-systems/
- Children and Divorce - HelpGuide.org
  https://www.helpguide.org/articles/parenting-family/children-and-divorce.htm
- Emotion Regulation and Parent Co-Regulation in Children
  https://www.ncbi.nlm.nih.gov/pmc/articles/PMC5352765/
- What Is Co-Regulation and What Does It Look Like
  https://turnaroundusa.org/what-is-co-regulation-and-what-does-it-look-like-in-the-classroom/
- 5 Key Benefits Of A Strong Parent - Teacher Relationship For
  https://www.linkedin.com/pulse/5-key-benefits-strong-parent-teacher-relationship-student
- Digital Citizenship | Common Sense Education
  https://www.commonsense.org/education/digital-citizenship
- Social Support, Family Functioning and Parenting
  https://www.ncbi.nlm.nih.gov/pmc/articles/PMC4233010/

- Co-Regulation From Birth Through Young Adulthood
  https://fpg.unc.edu/sites/fpg.unc.edu/files/resources/reports-and-policy-briefs/Co-RegulationFromBirthThroughYoungAdulthood.pdf
- Co-Regulation in Practice: Strategies for Practitioners Who
  https://www.acf.hhs.gov/opre/report/co-regulation-practice-strategies-practitioners-who-serve-youth-aged-14-24
- Emotional Intelligence and Mental Health in the Family
  https://www.ncbi.nlm.nih.gov/pmc/articles/PMC7503667/
- The emotional intelligence of today's parents – influences
  https://www.ncbi.nlm.nih.gov/pmc/articles/PMC10352801/

www.ingramcontent.com/pod-product-compliance
Lightning Source LLC
Chambersburg PA
CBHW051156120626
46547CB00012B/1090